MW00612736

Things God Hates,
Things God Loves

Things God Hates, Things God Loves

BECOME THE KIND OF PERSON
GOD WILL LOOK ON WITH FAVOR

GREG HERSHBERG

We enjoy hearing from our readers. Please contact us at www.anekopress.com/questions-comments with any questions, comments, or suggestions.

Cover Designer: Jonathan Lewis

Editors: Sheila Wilkinson and Ruth Clark

Aneko Press

www.anekopress.com

Aneko Press, Life Sentence Publishing, and our logos are trademarks of

Life Sentence Publishing, Inc.
203 E. Birch Street
P.O. Box 652
Abbotsford, WI 54405

RELIGION / Christian Living / Spiritual Growth

Paperback ISBN: 978-1-62245-887-5

eBook ISBN: 978-1-62245-888-2

10 9 8 7 6 5 4 3 2 1

Available where books are sold

CONTENTS

Preface ix

Ch. 1: The Heart of God 1

Ch. 2: The Man Whom God Favors 7

Ch. 3: God Hates a Haughty Look 17

Ch. 4: God Hates a Lying Tongue 25

Ch. 5: God Hates Hands That Shed Innocent Blood 33

Ch. 6: God Hates a Heart That Plots Wicked Schemes 39

Ch. 7: God Hates Feet That Are Swift in Running to Do Evil 45

Ch. 8: God Hates a False Witness Who Lies with Every Breath 53

Ch. 9: God Hates One Who Sows Discord among Brethren 61

Ch. 10: God Loves Mankind 67

Ch. 11: God Loves Sinners 75

Ch. 12: God Loves His Children 83

Ch. 13: God Loves Those Who Do What Is Right 91

Ch. 14: God Loves Those Who Obey His Word 97

Ch. 15: God Loves Those Who Treat Others Fairly 107

Ch. 16: God Loves a Cheerful Giver 119

Ch. 17: A Man after God's Heart 129

Ch. 18: The Gospel According to Isaiah 141

The Conclusion 153

About the Author 161

PREFACE

When I met the Lord on the Transfiguration Mount in Israel on October 9, 1989, I fell head over heels in love with Him. I say *met,* because I did in fact meet Him. Not only was it a legitimate encounter, but He also spoke with me. Was it an audible voice, or was it an internal voice? I don't know that, but what I do know is that I heard His voice, and I was forever changed.

At that time, I assumed that this is how everyone came to know the Lord, as I was a blank slate when it came to the things of God. I never looked back from that encounter, but found out later that this is exactly what Yeshua (Jesus) said to a would-be disciple in the gospel of Luke: *"No one who puts his hand to the plow and keeps looking back is fit to serve in the Kingdom of God"* (Luke 9:62 *Complete Jewish Bible* (CJB)). Yeshua told this would-be disciple that once he put his hand to the plow of discipleship, he must not look back; otherwise, he was not fit for the kingdom of God.

The expression, *Not fit for the kingdom* (Luke 9:62 NLT), does not refer to salvation but to service. It is not a question of *entrance* into the kingdom but of *service* in the kingdom after entering. No considerations of family or friends, though lawful in themselves, must be allowed to turn them aside from utter and complete surrender to Him. Messiah must reign in the heart without a rival. All other loves and all other loyalties must be secondary.

Not only did I not look back, but I also had this strong desire to know Him as best as I could. I can't explain it, except to say that I just had to satisfy it. I didn't have anyone in my life to direct me to the next step, so I began to read, or should I say devour, the Bible. Along with daily Bible reading, I also talked to God incessantly.

Since I met the Lord through an encounter, I assumed that He wanted to meet with me on a regular basis, so I began conversing with Him, although most of the conversation was me asking questions. As I read the Bible, I didn't understand what I was reading, so I asked a lot of questions. All these "conversations" with the Lord, unbeknownst to me, were actually developing an intimacy between Him and me.

I spent hours and hours a day reading the Bible and meditating on Scripture. I would read a verse several times, look up the words in the concordance, and ask God to help me to understand its meaning. It's been thirty-three years since I first met the Lord, and not much has changed as far as my approach to God is concerned. I still read the Bible regularly, and I still look up the words in the concordance. I do a lot of cross-referencing as well, as I have learned that Scripture must be read in context in order to interpret it correctly. And last but not least, I still talk with God often.

After traveling to all fifty states in America, as well as to over forty countries on six continents, I have met believers from all over the world. I have since grouped the body of Messiah into three basic categories, and I like to use the tabernacle in the wilderness to illustrate this. In the tabernacle, there were three compartments or sections. There was the outer courtyard, there was the Holy Place, and there was the holy of holies.

Some believers dwell in the outer courtyard. They did in fact enter into the kingdom through the correct door, Yeshua, and therefore they are in fact inside the kingdom. They came in poor in spirit. They acknowledged their own helplessness and relied on God's omnipotence. They sensed their spiritual need and found it supplied in the Lord, and they are overjoyed to be part of God's family. They live their lives in such a way as to honor the Lord for paying the ultimate price to save their souls.

Others are not satisfied to dwell in the outer courtyard. Although they are overjoyed at the price that was paid for their salvation, they want to go deeper. They tend to have a greater hunger and thirst for God's righteousness. These people have a passion for righteousness in their own lives; they long to see honesty, integrity, and justice in society; and they look for practical holiness in the body of Messiah. They want more of God, so they go behind the curtain and enter into the Holy Place.

Then there are those who want still more; they want to be as close to God as humanly possible. They tend to be a tad more purehearted. Their motives are unmixed, their thoughts are holy, and their conscience is clean. Their conscience is not clean from never sinning but from loving the Lord with their whole heart and repenting quickly when they do sin. They are more than willing to suffer for doing right, as their integrity and lifestyle condemns the ungodly world and brings out its hostility. They want to enter the holy of holies because they want more of God's presence.

You may be outside the kingdom, and you just want to come in. If that is your desire, please keep reading and you'll find out how to get there; I promise. Or, you may be inside the kingdom, and yet you have a desire to develop more of an intimate relationship with God. Please read on, and you'll find out how. Or, you may be close to God, and yet you have an insatiable desire to get closer still. Read on as well, and you can get there also. Whatever the case may be, the more we know what God hates, and the more we know what God loves, the more we can position ourselves to greater intimacy with Him. No view of God is complete unless it sees that God is capable of hatred as well as love. It was in this spirit that this book was birthed and written.

CHAPTER 1

THE HEART OF GOD

Growing up in a religious Jewish family and going to Hebrew school three days a week, as well as attending weekly Shabbat services gave me a good understanding of God in the abstract. I understood right from wrong in God's eyes, but I had no idea that God wanted a relationship with me. I never dreamed that I could have a close relationship with God, let alone get His attention. I thought that He was up in heaven, and we were down on earth, and our job was to obey His commands, and if we got out of line, His job was to "zap" us. Sadly enough, for me it was more about perfection than it was about connection. An impossible task, I may add.

Only after I had an encounter with the Lord did I realize He actually wanted to have a close, intimate relationship with me. I never heard of such a thing, and you can imagine how incredible and refreshing this revelation was for me. I was convinced that He already knew everything about me, but now I wanted to get to know everything about Him, or at least as much as I possibly could.

I wanted to know the heart of God. I wanted to know what made Him tick. I wanted to know what made Him happy and what made Him sad. I wanted to know what He expected of me and what I could expect of Him. In actuality, I wanted to know what He hated and what He loved. But how? I discovered that the more I read His Word and prayed, the more I would know Him – the more I would know His heart.

Isaiah is arguably the greatest of the Hebrew prophets. Correctly he has been called the Prince of Prophets. He wrote the longest, loveliest, and most messianic of all Old Testament prophecies. The meaning of Isaiah's name also gives the main theme of the book: "Salvation is from the Lord." The word *salvation* occurs twenty-six times in this prophecy and only seven times in all the other prophets put together. This theme also illustrates the unity of the book: Isaiah falls into two main sections that are agreed upon by most – chapters 1-39 and chapters 40-66. It is interesting how chapters 1-39 mirror the Old Testament and chapters 40-66 parallel the New Testament, even in the numbers: one chapter per Old Testament book and one chapter per New Testament book. Chapters 1-39 depict man's tremendous need for salvation, and chapters 40-66 give God's gracious provision for it.

Isaiah warned Israel that her lawlessness would be punished, and yet God in His infinite mercy and amazing grace would one day provide a Savior for both Jews and Gentiles. In the opening verses of the last chapter of the prophecy, we see the consummation of Israel's restoration:

> *"Heaven is my throne," says* ADONAI, *"and the earth is my footstool. What kind of house could you build for me? What sort of place could you devise for my rest? Didn't I myself make all these things? This is how they all came to be," says* ADONAI. *"The kind of person on whom I look with favor is one with a poor and humble spirit, who trembles at my word."*
> (Isaiah 66:1-2)

These words of Isaiah were written to the unrepentant people of Israel. They need not think that in their condition they can please God by building a temple for Him. After all, He is the universal Creator and Owner, enthroned in heaven with the earth as His footstool. It's like God is saying, "I sit on top of the heaven of heavens, and planet earth is my ottoman. Do you really think you can build a big-enough house for me to dwell in?" The question is obviously rhetorical, so the prophet goes on to tell us that the dwelling place God desires is the heart of a person who is humble and contrite and trembles at His Word.

The word *humble* comes to us from the Hebrew word *aw-nee,* and it means "afflicted and needy." The word *contrite* comes to us from the Hebrew word *nabat,* and it means "smitten and dejected." God is not saying that we have to be depressed and down-and-out in order for Him to look upon us with favor. Rather, He is saying that we need to be cognizant and conscious of our great need of Him. We have to come to the realization that we are dependent on Him and not the other way around. We have to realize that we desperately need Him, because apart from Him, we can do nothing.

John 15:5 says, *"I am the vine and you are the branches. Those who stay united with me, and I with them, are the ones who bear much fruit; because apart from me you can't do a thing."* Messiah Yeshua Himself is the Vine; believers are the vine branches. It is not a question of the branch living its life for the Vine, but simply of letting the life of the Vine flow out through the branches. Sometimes we pray, "Lord, help me to live my life for You." It would be better to pray, "Lord, live out Your life through me." Without Yeshua, we can do nothing. A vine branch has one great purpose, and that is to bear fruit. It is useless for making furniture or for building homes. It does not even make good firewood. But it is good for fruit bearing, as long as it abides in the vine. So, we have to come to the realization that we need Him!

A vine branch has one great purpose, and that is to bear fruit.

Then the Lord goes on to say in Isaiah 66:2 that not only do we need to be dependent on Him and desperate for Him, but we also need to *tremble* at His Word. The word *tremble* comes to us from the Hebrew word *khaw-rade*. This verse does not mean to literally shake from fear or weakness from the reading or the hearing of God's Word. What it does mean is that those who tremble at God's Word are those who reverence His commands. The spiritual connotation of trembling at God's Word is simply to love what He loves and to hate what He hates.

The Lord says that He will *look with favor* to the one who is humble and contrite and who trembles at His Word. This word *look* in the Hebrew is *naw-bat,* and it is a primitive root meaning "to regard, to consider, or to pay attention to." In actuality, the Lord is saying that the dependent person who hates what He hates and loves what He loves is the one He pays attention to with favor.

It was mind-blowing when I realized that the almighty Creator and Sustainer of the universe would pay attention to us with favor. To think that we could get God to notice us with favor is amazing and overwhelmingly beautiful, to say the least.

John 14:8-9 says, *Philip said to him, "Lord, show us the Father, and it will be enough for us." Yeshua replied to him, "Have I been with you so long without your knowing me, Philip? Whoever has seen me has seen the Father; so how can you say, 'Show us the Father'?"*

Philip wanted the Lord to give him some special revelation of the Father, and that would be all he would ask. He did not understand that everything the Lord was and did and said was a revelation of the Father. Yeshua patiently corrected him. Philip had been with the Lord for a long time. He was one of the first disciples to be called (John 1:43). Yet the full truth of Messiah's deity and of his unity with the Father had not yet dawned on him. He did not know that when he looked at Yeshua, he was looking at One who perfectly displayed the Father. John 14:10-11 says, *"Don't you believe that I am united with the Father, and the Father united with me? What I am telling you, I am not saying on my own initiative; the Father living in me is doing his own works. Trust me, that I am united with the Father, and the Father united with me."*

The words, *I am united with the Father, and the Father united with me* describe the closeness of the union between the Father and the Son. They are separate persons, yet they are one as to attributes and will. We should not be discouraged if we cannot understand this. No mortal mind will ever fully understand the Godhead. We must give God credit for knowing things that we can never know. If we fully understood Him, we would be as great as He is, and that is ridiculous, to say the least. We will never fully understand or know God perfectly; however, we can know Him better than we do, and this entails getting to know Yeshua. I thought if I read the Gospels over and over again, I would gain a greater understanding of the Father through the Son and come to know the heart of God.

There was an acronym in the Christian world the year I got saved known as WWJD. It was based off a book first published in 1896, by Charles Monroe Sheldon, entitled *In His Steps: What Would Jesus Do?* The book sold over fifty million copies. It was a brilliant move to help foster living like Yeshua did. I wanted to know how He lived and what He did and then try to live and do as He did – in other words, WDJD, What Did Jesus Do, and then do likewise. I believed that the more I emulated the life of Yeshua, the more I would be the kind of man that God chooses to use.

CHAPTER 2

THE MAN WHOM GOD FAVORS

Adonai, who can rest in your tent? Who can live on your holy mountain? Those who live a blameless life, who behave uprightly, who speak truth from their hearts and keep their tongues from slander; who never do harm to others or seek to discredit neighbors; who look with scorn on the vile, but honor those who fear Adonai; who hold to an oath, no matter the cost; who refuse usury when they lend money and refuse a bribe to damage the innocent. Those who do these things never will be moved. (Psalm 15)

The individual that God favors (chooses) as His companion is the subject of Psalm 15. Although it does not say so in the psalm, the basic qualification for entrance into God's kingdom is being born again. Apart from the new birth, no one can see or enter the kingdom (John 3:3). This birth from above is experienced by grace, through faith, and takes place completely apart from any meritorious works on man's part (Ephesians 2:8-9).

Taken by itself, the psalm seems to imply that salvation is somehow connected to man's righteous character or noble deeds. But taken with the rest of Scripture, it can only mean that the kind of faith that saves is the kind of faith that results in a life of holiness.

> *What good is it, my brothers, if someone claims to have faith but has no actions to prove it? Is such "faith" able to save him? Suppose a brother or sister is without clothes and daily food, and someone says to him, "Shalom!* [Peace] *Keep warm and eat hearty!" without giving him what he needs, what good does it do? Thus, faith by itself, unaccompanied by actions, is dead.* (James 2:14-17)

James insists that a faith that does not result in good works cannot save. There are two keys that help with the understanding of these verses. First of all, James does not say, "What good is it if a man has faith"; he says, *What good is it, . . . if someone **claims** to have faith* (emphasis added). In other words, it is not a question of a man who truly *has* faith and yet is not saved. James is describing the man who has nothing but a profession of faith. He says he has faith, but nothing about his life indicates it. This is a spiritual syndrome that some have fallen prey to. I use the acronym HTLW to describe what James is referring to, nothing other than the High Talk Low Walk syndrome. As the saying goes, "Talk is cheap."

The second helpful key is brought out in the *Complete Jewish Bible* where the verse closes with the question, *Is such "faith" able to save him?* Or as it is stated in the New American Standard Bible (NASB), *Can that faith save him?* In other words, can that kind of faith save? If it is asked what kind of faith James is referring to, the answer is found in the first part of the verse. He is speaking about a say-so faith that is not backed up by good works. Such a faith is worthless. It is all words and nothing more. The person is a professor as opposed to a possessor. The futility of words without deeds is also illustrated in James 2:15-16 – *Suppose a brother or sister is without clothes and daily food, and someone says to him, "Shalom! Keep warm and eat hearty!" without giving him what he needs, what good does it do?* We are introduced to two people here. One has neither adequate daily food nor clothing. The other has both but is not willing to share them. Professing great generosity, the latter basically says to his poor brother, "Go and put on some clothing and eat a good meal." But he doesn't raise a little finger to make this possible. What good are such words? They are positively worthless! They neither satisfy the appetite nor provide warmth for the body.

> A faith without works is not real faith at all. It is only a matter of words.

A faith without works is not real faith at all. It is only a matter of words. James is not saying that we are saved by faith plus works. To hold such a view would be to dishonor the finished work of Messiah Yeshua. If we are saved by faith plus works, then there would be two saviors: Yeshua and ourselves. But the New Testament is very clear that Yeshua is the one and only Savior. James is emphasizing that we are not saved by a faith of words only but also by that kind of faith that results in a life of good works.

In other words, works are not the root of salvation but the fruit of salvation; they are not the cause but the effect. Faith produces the works; works are evidence of the faith. James 2:18 says, *But someone will say that you have faith and I have actions. Show me this faith of yours without the actions, and I will show you my faith by my actions!*

True faith and good works are inseparable. James shows this by giving us a bit from a debate between two men. The first man, who is genuinely saved, is the speaker. The second professes to have faith, but he does not demonstrate that faith by good works. The first is heard delivering an unanswerable challenge to the other. We might paraphrase the conversation this way: "Yes," the first man may correctly and justifiably say, "you say you *have faith*, but you do not have works to demonstrate it. I claim that faith must be backed up by a life of works. Prove to me that you have faith without a life of good works. You cannot do it. Faith is invisible. The only way others can know you have faith is by a life that demonstrates it. *I will show you my faith by my actions!*" The key to this verse lies in the word *show:* To show faith apart from works is impossible.

Like James in his epistle, David says that genuine faith in the Lord results in the kind of good works described in Psalm 15. In other words, faith without works is dead, or as the saying goes, "Actions speak louder than words." For instance, James 1:27

says, *The religious observance that God the Father considers pure and faultless is this: to care for orphans and widows in their distress and to keep oneself from being contaminated by the world.* What God is looking for is the practical type of godliness that takes a compassionate interest in others and keeps one's own life clean. James praises the man who visits needy orphans and widows and who keeps himself unspotted from the world. In other words, the practical outworking of the new birth is found in acts of grace and a walk of separation. It is operating in practical love and practical holiness.

Psalm 15 does not give a complete catalog of the virtues of the citizen of heaven. The portrait is suggestive but certainly not exhaustive. It gives us an overall picture of the man God chooses to look at with favor. At the beginning of Psalm 15, the question is asked, ADONAI, *who can rest in your tent? Who can live on your holy mountain?* The answer follows in the rest of the psalm.

Verse 2 says the men God chooses are *those who live a blameless life, who behave uprightly, who speak truth from their hearts.* First of all, the man whom God chooses walks with integrity. The word *blameless* is *taw-meem* in the Hebrew. It is used interchangeably in other versions of the Bible with the word *uprightly*. It means "sincere, undefiled, and sound." Therefore, the man of integrity is a man of moral soundness. He is complete, well-rounded, and balanced. It does not mean that he never falls short of God's glory, because even though our sins are washed away when we are born again, our sin nature is not. Therefore, at times, we still sin. The key is to allow the Holy Spirit to empower us to live a life of righteousness, and if and when we do fall, to repent quickly and get back in the race.

Second, the man whom God chooses does what is right. He is careful to maintain a conscience that is void of offense. He would rather go to heaven with a good conscience than stay on earth with a bad one. You can depend on this man to tell the truth from his heart. He would rather die than lie. His word is his bond. His yes means yes, and his no means no. This quality is hard to find in the day in which we live. Many today claim that there is no absolute truth, which we know is absolutely not true, biblically speaking of course. For Yeshua said in John 14:6, *"I AM . . . the Truth."* He is not just one who teaches the truth, He *is* the Truth. He is the embodiment of truth. Those who have Messiah have the Truth, which is not found anywhere else.

Verse 3 says the men whom God chooses *keep their tongues from slander; who never do harm to others or seek to discredit neighbors.* The man whom God chooses does not attack with his tongue the character or reputation of a person who is not present. He won't gossip about others. Slander and mudslinging never get past his lips. He disciplines his tongue to edify instead of assassinate. He does no evil to his neighbor; his whole desire is to help to encourage and to instruct. When he hears some juicy tidbit of scandal about his friend, he not only lets it die right there, but he also confronts it, and is always dependable to not repeat it to anyone.

It seems that defamation of character has become a national pastime in our society. Defamation and mudslinging are not new, but they appear to be more and more prevalent in today's world. With the advent of the computer and social media, defamation has become more far-reaching and much more damaging.

Sadly enough, this is becoming more and more commonplace and customary today. This practice is an integral part of the evil world system that we find ourselves living in. But the man whom God chooses will have nothing to do with this evil, for he is in this world but not of this world (John 17:14-16). We should remember this when we are tempted to engage in some worldly pastime or to enter into worldly associations where the name of Yeshua is unwelcome.

Verse 4 says the men whom God chooses are those *who look with scorn on the vile, but honor those who fear ADONAI.* Moral distinctions are not blurred in the vision of the man whom God chooses. He discerns between sin and righteousness, darkness and light, evil and good. He despises a vile person in the sense that he outspokenly witnesses against his ungodliness. And although he despises his vileness, he seeks his deliverance. In other words, he hates the sin but loves the sinner. On the other hand, he identifies himself in open approval with everyone in the household of faith. Once he has made a promise, he stands by it, even if it results in financial loss. A believer, for example, might agree to sell his house for $175,000, but before the papers are signed, he finds he could have sold the house for $200,000. However, he has given his word to the first buyer, and he keeps his contract.

> *The man God chooses hates the sin but loves the sinner.*

Verse 5 says the men whom God chooses will *refuse usury when they lend money and refuse a bribe to damage the innocent.* The person God looks upon with grace does not lend his money with interest, that is, to another member of God's family. He does not look for financial gain from a brother in the faith. Finally, the righteous man does not take a bribe against the innocent. He hates the perversion of justice and disproves the old saying "that everyone has his price."

Psalm 15 ends on the following note: *Those who do these things never will be moved.* The psalmist is saying that the man with the aforementioned character traits is the type of person that will be attractive to God and who lives for God in time and for eternity; come to think of it, no one else would be comfortable in God's presence.

Proverbs 12:3 says, *No one is made secure by wickedness, but the roots of the righteous will never be moved.* Lives that are dominated by wickedness have no stability. They are like the seed that fell on rocky places (Matthew 13:5-6); the earth was shallow, and because they had no root, the seeds quickly withered away. A righteous man has his root deep in God. He is able to stand when the storms of life blow.

An actual list of seven things that the Lord hates is in the book of Proverbs. But if God is love, how can He hate? First John 4:8 says, *Those who do not love, do not know God; because God is love.* It does not say that God loves. That is true, but John is emphasizing that God *is* love. Love is His nature. There is no love in the true sense but that which finds its source in Him.

While it is true that God is love, it is not the whole truth. I believe God's love is overemphasized by many today, while His righteousness and holiness fade away. Proverbs tells us that there are in fact things that the Lord hates: *There are six things ADONAI hates, seven which he detests: a haughty look, a lying tongue, hands that shed innocent blood, a heart that plots wicked schemes, feet swift in running to do evil, a false witness who lies with every breath, and him who sows strife among brothers* (Proverbs 6:16-19).

The things that characterize the wicked man in verses 12-15 are those hated by God in verses 16-19: *A scoundrel, a vicious man, lives by crooked speech, winking his eyes, shuffling his feet, pointing with his fingers. With deceit in his heart, he is always plotting evil and sowing discord. Therefore disaster suddenly overcomes him; unexpectedly, he is broken beyond repair.*

The formula, *six things . . . [yes] seven,* may mean that the list is specific but not exhaustive. Or it may indicate that the seventh is worst of all. Whatever the case, as children of the Most High God, we need to better understand the things that our heavenly Father hates. If they are detestable to Him, then they should be detestable to us as well. Yeshua and the Father are one (John 10:30); therefore, what the Father hates, Yeshua hates. And since we are called to be like Yeshua, we need to hate those things as well. These seven things are not to be taken lightly by the body of Messiah. We must not only know them theoretically, but we must also apply them in a practical sense in our everyday lives. God isn't just looking for creed, but character. He isn't just interested in our beliefs, but our behavior too.

God isn't just interested in our beliefs, but our behavior too.

Therefore, it is imperative that we, as the children of God, delve into these seven things that our heavenly Father detests, in order to gain a better understanding of His heart. Once we better understand His heart, we can then become men and women after His heart. The more we hate the things God hates, the more we will get His attention, and He will look upon us with favor.

CHAPTER 3

GOD HATES A HAUGHTY LOOK

God hates a haughty look. The word *haughty* is synonymous with the word *pride*. It comes to us from the Hebrew word *rum*. It means "to rise up, to be lofty, and to be exalted." I don't know if this list of things that God hates in Proverbs 6:16-19 is in some kind of order of importance, but I have to say that pride is the father of all sins. Pride is dust deifying itself. In fact, some people are so vain that they have to be the central figure in everything. If they go to a christening, they want to be the baby. If they go to a wedding, they want to be the bride. If they go to a funeral, they want to be the deceased. However, God should be front and center, and high and lifted up (Isaiah 57:15).

Psalm 19:13-14 says, *Who can discern unintentional sins? Cleanse me from hidden faults. Also keep your servant from presumptuous sins, so that they won't control me.* When we think about how holy, just, and perfect the law of the Lord is, we realize what failures we are, and we exclaim with David, *Who can discern unintentional sins?* Who can recall the number of times he has departed from such a law? As the Scriptures expose us to ourselves and convict us of sins we were previously unaware of, we are prompted to pray for forgiveness from faults hidden to ourselves and even to others, but not to God. Sin is sin, even if we are unaware of it. So, our confession should always cover hidden sins. The psalm teaches us to pray not only for cleansing from unknown sins but also for preservation from presumptuous sins, that is, from sins that are born of pride and self-confidence. Let us never forget that it was pride that led Lucifer's original rebellion against God.

Psalm 103:10 says, *He has not treated us as our sins deserve or paid us back for our offenses.* If we received what we deserve to receive, we would be in hell forever. But God's mercy is demonstrated in that He does not give us what we deserve. There are sins of commission, sins of omission, premeditated sins, sins we are not aware of, sins that we don't think are sins, and secret sins. When we consider all the vastness of our sins, it is utterly amazing that not only did God not treat us as our sins deserve, but our sins also were paid for by another at the cross of Golgotha.

With that being said, there is a situation where God draws His proverbial line in the sand, and it has to do with His glory. *I am Adonai; that is my name. I yield my glory to no one else* (Isaiah 42:8). The Lord will not share His greatness with another. In God's economy, the humble are bestowed grace, but the proud are resisted. Why is pride so dangerously sinful? Because pride is giving ourselves credit for something that God has accomplished. We live in a society where when things go well, man takes the credit, and when things go awry, God gets the blame.

Pride is essentially self-worship. Anything that we accomplish would not be possible were it not for God enabling us to do so. First Corinthians 4:7 says, *After all, what makes you so special? What do you have that you didn't receive as a gift? And if in fact it was a gift, why do you boast as if it weren't?* If one believing teacher happens to be more gifted than another, it is only because God made him so. Everything he has, he has received from the Lord. In fact, it is true of all of us that everything we have has been given to us by God. That being the case, why should we be proud or puffed up? Our talents and gifts are not the results of our own cleverness. This is why we give God the glory, for he alone deserves it.

> *Why is pride so dangerously sinful? Because pride is giving ourselves credit for something that God has accomplished.*

I have traveled all over the world, and I have seen some magnificent architectural structures. Yet in all my travels, I have never heard the hammer or the nail say, "Look what I've built." The structure is built by the builder himself. How dare the clay take the glory from the potter master. *But now, ADONAI, you are our father; we are the clay, you are our potter; and we are all the work of your hands* (Isaiah 64:8). It would be like man taking the credit for the Grand Canyon.

"The scornful he scorns, but gives grace to the humble." (Proverbs 3:34)

But the grace he gives is greater, which is why it says, "God opposes the arrogant, but to the humble he gives grace." (James 4:6)

Likewise, you who are less experienced, submit to leaders. Further, all of you should clothe yourselves in humility toward one another, because God opposes the arrogant, but to the humble he gives grace. (1 Peter 5:5)

All believers should be clothed with humility; it is a great virtue. Moffatt says, "Put on the apron of humility."[1] Very appropriate, since the apron is the badge of a servant. A missionary to India once said, "If I were to pick out two phrases necessary for spiritual growth, I would pick out these: 'I don't know' and 'I am sorry.' And both phrases are the evidence of deep humility." Imagine a congregation where all the members have this humble spirit, where they esteem others better than themselves, and where they outdo each other in performing the menial tasks. Such a congregation need not be imaginary; it could, and should, be an actuality.

If there were no other reason for being humble, this would be enough: *"God resists the proud, but gives grace to the humble"* (1 Peter 5:5 NKJV; cf. Proverbs 3:34). Think of it, the almighty God opposed to our pride and determined to break it, contrasted with the almighty God powerless to resist a broken and

---

1   James Moffatt, *The Moffatt Translation of the Bible* (Chicago: The University of Chicago Press, 1922), 1 Peter 5:5.

a contrite heart (Psalm 51:17). The Bible tells us repeatedly to humble ourselves before the Lord. I can tell you from experience that it is far better to humble ourselves than to have the Lord humble us.

Pride was the parent sin of the universe. Satan himself was cast out of heaven because of pride.

> *"How did you come to fall from the heavens, morning star, son of the dawn? How did you come to be cut to the ground, conqueror of nations? You thought to yourself, 'I will scale the heavens, I will raise my throne above God's stars. I will sit on the Mount of Assembly far away in the north. I will rise past the tops of the clouds, I will make myself like the Most High.' Instead you are brought down to Sh'ol, to the uttermost depths of the pit."* (Isaiah 14:12-15)

Satan had the selfish audacity to attempt to replace God Himself as the rightful ruler of the universe, but he will be cast down to hell in the final judgment of God. For those who rise up in defiance against God, there is nothing ahead but disaster. *"I will arise against them," says* ADONAI-*Tzva'ot* [The Lord of Heaven's armies]. *"I will cut off from Bavel name and remnant, offshoot and offspring," says* ADONAI (Isaiah 14:22). When it comes to God's kingdom, we are always able to see much further on our knees!

The proud will be humbled, but the humble will be honored (Proverbs 29:23). A proud man can be sure of being brought low. The humble man is elevated to a place of honor. Professor

Smith was climbing the Weisshorn. When near the top, the guide stood aside to permit the traveler to have the honor of reaching the summit first. Exhilarated by the view, forgetful of the fierce gale that was blowing, he sprang up and stood erect on the summit. The guide pulled him down, exclaiming, "On your knees, sir; you are not safe there except on your knees." Life's summits, whether of knowledge, of love, or of worldly success, are full of perils. It's always best to approach all things in humility, and avoid being swept away in our pride by the broom of God!

Proverbs 16:18 says, *Pride goes before destruction, and arrogance before failure.* A tall tree attracts lightning. So God puts down those who are conceited. Stuck-up people usually suffer some humiliating experience designed to deflate their ego. It takes only a small pin to prick a large balloon.

A tall tree attracts lightning. So God puts down those who are conceited.

Proverbs 11:2 says, *First comes pride, then disgrace; but with the humble is wisdom.* First pride, then a fall; then comes shame connected with the fall. But to be humble and down-to-earth reduces the danger of stumbling.

Recently I spent a relaxing day at the beach with one of my children. The beach is a favorite spot of mine to connect with God and enjoy His handiwork. It always amazes me at how the waves bow at the Lord's feet. Even inanimate creation knows its Creator. As I meditated on the Lord's goodness, a young bodybuilder approached the jetty with a photographer by his side. He began to "pose" on top of the jetty as the photographer took pictures. As he was doing that, he slipped and fell back on the rock. Thank God, he was not seriously injured, but my first thought was, "Pride comes before the fall."

Proverbs 18:12 says, *Before being ruined, a person's heart is proud; before being honored, a person must be humble.* Pride has one foot in the grave and another on a banana skin. Humility walks securely toward honor. William Law draws the contrast sharply: "Look not at pride only as an unbecoming temper, nor at humility as a decent virtue – one is all hell and the other all heaven."[2]

In the Gospel of Luke chapter 9, the disciples not only expected the glorious kingdom to be ushered in shortly, but they also aspired to positions of greatness in the kingdom. Already they were arguing among themselves as to who would be greatest, so Yeshua gave the following answer: *But Yeshua, knowing the thoughts of their hearts, took a child, stood him beside himself, and said to them, "Whoever welcomes this child in my name welcomes me, and whoever welcomes me welcomes the One who sent me. In other words, the one who is least among you all – this is the one who is great"* (Luke 9:47-48).

Knowing the question that was agitating them, Yeshua brought a little child beside Him and explained that anyone who received a little child in His name received Him. At first glance, this does not seem to have any connection with the question of who was the greatest among the disciples. Though not obvious, the connection seems to be this: true greatness is seen in a loving care for the little ones, for those who are helpless, for those whom the world passes by. Thus, when Yeshua said that the least among you will be great, He was referring to

---

2   William Law, "The First Dialogue between Academicus, Rusticus and Theophilus; at which Humanus was present," *The Second Part of the Spirit of PRAYER* (London: Printed for J. Richardson, 1750), Pryr-2.1-73.

the one who humbled himself to associate with believers who are nondescript, insignificant, and despised.

In Matthew 18, the Lord said that the greatest in the kingdom of heaven is the one who humbles himself like a little child. In Luke, it is a manner of identifying oneself with the lowliest among God's children. In both cases, it involves taking a place of humility, as the Savior Himself did.

CHAPTER 4

GOD HATES A LYING TONGUE

God hates a lying tongue. The word *lying* is the Hebrew word *sheh-ker*, and it means "to deceive," and it refers to that which betrays someone. The tongue was created to glorify God, so to lie is to pervert its use for that which is despicable. Is it ever right for a believer to lie? The answer is that God cannot lie, and He cannot give the privilege to anyone else.

The Hebrew midwives during the time that Moses was born are credited with saving many lives in their defiance of the king of Egypt and his order to kill all male Hebrew babies. The midwives, whose names were Shifrah and Pu'ah (Exodus 1:15), kept the babies alive. When brought before the king to explain their actions, *the midwives answered Pharaoh, "It's because the Hebrew women aren't like the Egyptian women — they go into labor and give birth before the midwife arrives"* (Exodus 1:19).

The rewards given to the midwives in terms of a flourishing family life were granted not for their lies but for their humanity: *Indeed, because the midwives feared God, he made them founders of families* (Exodus 1:21).

This is not to say that the end justified the means. But in a world as charged with sin and its effects as ours has become, it may be that obedience to greater duties is possible only at the cost of obedience to lesser ones. They were commended for their fear of the Lord. The Bible is clear that lying is a sin and is displeasing to God.

Proverbs 12:22 says, *Lying lips are an abomination to* A DONAI, *but those who deal faithfully are his delight.* God hates lying. How careful we should be about shading the truth, and telling white lies, exaggerations, and half-truths! A sure way of bringing delight to God's heart is by being absolutely honest and trustworthy.

The first sin in this world involved a lie told to Eve. In fact, satan himself is known as the father of lies. When referring to satan, the Bible says, *"You belong to your father, satan, and you want to carry out your father's desires. From the start he was a murderer, and he has never stood by the truth, because there is no truth in him. When he tells a lie, he is speaking in character; because he is a liar – indeed the inventor of the lie!"* (John 8:44).

Here the Lord Yeshua openly tells them the devil was their father. This did not mean that they had been born of the devil in the way believers are born of God. Rather, it meant that they were children of the devil by imitation. They showed their relationship to the devil by living the way he lived. Wanting to carry out his desires expresses the intention or tendency of their hearts. The devil was a murderer from the beginning. He brought death to Adam and the entire human race. Not only was he a murderer, but he was a liar as well. He did not stand in the truth, because there is no truth in him. When he told a lie, he was merely speaking from his own character. In other words, how do you know the devil is lying? Because his lips are moving. Lies formed a part of his very existence.

Wanting to carry out satan's desires expresses the intention or tendency of their hearts.

Lying would be following after satan and being a chip off his old evil block. We are called to be children of the Most High God and should therefore reflect His character.

The Ten Commandments beautifully sum up how we are to conduct ourselves as children of God. The Ten Commandments given to Moses include: *"Do not give false evidence against your neighbor"* (Exodus 20:16).

In the early body of Messiah, Ananias and Sapphira lied regarding a donation in order to make themselves look more generous than they really were. Peter's rebuke is stern: *"Ananias, why has satan filled your heart to lie to the Holy Spirit?"* (Acts 5:3 NASB). God's judgment was sterner; the couple died as a result of their sin of lying (Acts 5:1-11).

Colossians 3:9 says, *Never lie to one another; because you have stripped away the old self, with its ways.* Lying is listed in 1 Timothy 1:9-11 as something practiced by the lawless. Furthermore, liars will be among those judged in the end: *"But as for the cowardly, the untrustworthy, the vile, the murderers, the sexually immoral, those involved with the occult and with drugs, idol-worshippers, and all liars — their destiny is the lake burning with fire and sulfur, the second death"* (Revelation 21:8).

In contrast, God never lies. *God, who does not lie, promised that life before the beginning of time* (Titus 1:2). He is the source of truth. It is impossible for God to lie. *"God is not a human who lies or a mortal who changes his mind. When he says something, he will do it; when he makes a promise, he will fulfill it"* (Numbers 23:19).

Yeshua called Himself the Way, the Truth, and the Life (John 14:6), and He expects those who follow Him to be people of truth. The truth is to be expressed in love: *Instead, speaking the truth in love, we will in every respect grow up into him who is the head, the Messiah* (Ephesians 4:15), offering hope to those seeking redemption from the lies of the world. If we want to grow in the body of Messiah, there is the necessity of doctrinal adherence, but we must speak this truth in love. There can be no compromise as to the fundamentals of the faith.

There are major benefits to being honest. A major component in developing moral character is honesty, which helps in developing good attributes like kindness, discipline, truthfulness, moral integrity, and more. Lying, cheating, lack of trust, stealing, greed, and other immoral attributes have no part in honesty. It is very hard to overcome the reputation of a liar.

Proverbs 11:20 says, *The crooked-hearted are an abomination to Adonai, but those sincere in their ways are his delight.* As far as the Lord is concerned, a false heart is hateful and repulsive. He likes the person who is straightforward. No view of God is complete unless it sees that He is capable of hatred as well as love. A blameless heart, on the other hand, is His delight.

Throughout history and many civilizations, our moral laws are surprisingly similar from one culture to another. Honesty is universally esteemed, whereas lying is universally condemned. It has been said that it is difficult to tell the truth because of the potential repercussions. We may be afraid someone will think less of us if we tell the truth; we may lose a business deal, or we may even incur a fine or a jail sentence.

I wholeheartedly disagree with the position that it is hard to tell the truth. It is only hard to tell the truth because lying has become our natural mode of behavior. I believe it is always better to admit our shortcomings and simply endure the consequences rather than live inauthentically or in fear of being found out. Not to mention that it is much more difficult to remember a lie than to remember the truth, which is one of the forms of bondage from telling lies, along with the bondage of ignorance, error, and sin. Those who know Messiah Yeshua know the truth; they walk in the light and are led by the Holy Spirit. Let the truth set you free!

One has to be careful when it comes to the willingness to lie. Getting caught in a lie often destroys relationships. Lying has consequences. When someone finds out you have lied, it affects how that person deals with you forever. If your spouse lies, you may be able to work it out, but an employer is not likely to forgive. For that matter, most people are very unforgiving in general. If caught in a lie, you can get the reputation of being a liar and forever be branded as someone who cannot be trusted. This could mar a relationship forever.

Why do people lie? Psychologists tell us that lying allows a person to establish perceived control over a situation by manipulating it. Lying is a defense mechanism that seemingly prevents them from being vulnerable, that is, to not open up and reveal their true self to another person. Another theory is that most people lie in order to make themselves look better, to avoid hurting people's feelings, or to gain social status in some way. Lying is very problematic, as it paves the way for more and bigger lies.

In a new study conducted at the University College London, researchers told participants that overestimating the number of pennies in a jar would lead to personal

Lying is very problematic, as it paves the way for more and bigger lies.

gain. Participants' brains were scanned for activity during their responses. When they first began exaggerating the number of pennies in the jar, their amygdala, the brain's built-in gauge of right and wrong, responded strongly in reaction to their dishonesty. But as their exaggerations increased, the response of their amygdala decreased, showing that the brain becomes desensitized to repetitive dishonesty.

So, with every lie a person tells, the brain essentially feels less and less guilty or ashamed, which can lead to larger and more frequent lies. Senior author of the study, Tali Sharot, PhD, told *ScienceDaily,* "When we lie for personal gain, our amygdala produces a negative feeling that limits the extent to which we are prepared to lie. However, this response fades as we continue to lie, and the more it falls, the bigger our lies become. This may become a 'slippery slope,'" Sharot adds, "where small acts of dishonesty escalate into more significant lies."[3]

---

3   University College London, "*How lying takes our brains down a 'slippery slope'*: Telling small lies desensitizes our brains to the associated negative emotions and may encourage us to tell bigger lies in future." ScienceDaily: www.sciencedaily.com/releases/2016/10/161024134012.htm (August 16, 2022).

Therefore, lying only leads to more and bigger lies.

Revelation 22:14-15 reads: *How blessed are those who wash their robes, so that they have the right to eat from the Tree of Life and go through the gates into the city! Outside are the homosexuals, those involved with the occult and with drugs, the sexually immoral, murderers, idol-worshippers, and everyone who loves and practices falsehood.*

Strong language, to say the least. We need to retrain our brains so that honesty is always the best policy. Your motto should be: "If you don't want to know the truth, then don't ask me." Be honest, for this pleases the Lord.

CHAPTER 5

GOD HATES HANDS THAT SHED INNOCENT BLOOD

Why does God hate hands that shed innocent blood? Because every human life is of infinite value to Him. He proved this by paying an infinite price at Golgotha for our redemption. The institution of capital punishment in Genesis 9:6, where God states, *"Whoever sheds human blood, by a human being will his own blood be shed; for God made human beings in his image,"* reflects God's attitude toward murder. Let's bear in mind that the institution of capital punishment presupposes the establishment of governmental authority.

It would be chaos if anyone and everyone avenged a murder. Only duly appointed governments may do so. The New Testament perpetuates capital punishment when it says concerning the government: *For he is God's servant, there for your benefit. But if you do what is wrong, be afraid! Because it is not for nothing that he holds the power of the sword; for he is God's servant, there as an avenger to punish wrongdoers* (Romans 13:4).

The ruler, whether president, governor, mayor, or judge, is a minister of God in the sense that he is a servant and representative of the Lord. He may not know God personally, but he is still the Lord's man officially. As servants of God, rulers are expected to promote the good of the people, their security, tranquility, and general welfare. If any man insists on breaking the law, he can expect to pay for it, because the government has the authority to bring him to trial and punish him. In the expression, *He holds the power of the sword,* the word *sword* is not just a harmless symbol of power; a scepter would have served that purpose. The sword seems to speak of the ultimate power of the ruler – that is, to inflict capital punishment. So it will not do to say that capital punishment was for the Old Testament era only and not for the New Testament times. Romans 13:4 is a statement in the New Testament that implies that the government has the authority to take the life of a capital offender.

God is the God of the living, and life is very precious to Him. The sixth commandment of the Decalogue says, *"Do not murder"* (Exodus 20:13). This refers specifically to murder and not to capital punishment or to manslaughter. The command teaches respect for human life. The King James Version (KJV) of the Bible renders the sixth commandment in Exodus 20:13 and Deuteronomy 5:17 as *Thou shalt not kill.* This wording gives the impression that it is always wrong to take a human life, with no exceptions.

That is a wrong impression, for the Bible elsewhere allows for the execution of certain criminals (Genesis 9:6), and killing in the context of warfare (1 Chronicles 19:18). So, the command *Thou shalt not kill* cannot be taken in an absolute sense. In fact, the KJV's wording of *Thou shalt not kill* is far too broad and desperately in need of clarification. Nearly all modern translations correctly render the original Hebrew wording as *You shall not commit murder* (unjustified, deliberate homicide).

The Old Testament uses over half a dozen different Hebrew words for the taking of a human life. In Exodus 20:13, the Hebrew word used is *raw-tsakh,* which means "murder." It is the same word that the KJV correctly renders elsewhere as *murder* or *murderer,* including all eleven times that *raw-tsakh* appears in Numbers 35:17-31. Oddly enough, when they came to the sixth commandment, the KJV translators chose to translate the word as *kill* instead of *murder. Thou shalt not kill* is an incorrect and inconsistent translation.

That mistranslation has created needless confusion and personal moral conflict for centuries. Believers have debated with each other – and struggled in their own minds – over whether to serve in the military during wartime, to use deadly force as a police officer, or even to protect their own families from homicidal attacks. It's unfortunately true that protecting a nation, protecting society, and protecting loved ones sometimes requires *killing,* but that is different from *murder.*

The command *Do not murder* does not apply to justified killing in the course of one's duty. The mistranslation of Exodus 20:13 has also caused believers and skeptics alike to question the reliability of the Bible and the character and justness of God. After all, after commanding the Israelites not to kill anyone, God orders them to kill criminals for capital crimes (Exodus 21:12-29), Israelites who worshipped the gods of Moab (Numbers 25:1-8), all Midianite males and non-virgin females (Numbers 31:1-18), and the pagan societies of Canaan (Deuteronomy 2:30-36; Joshua 6; 1 Samuel 15:1-3). Capital punishment for the crime of murder was, in fact, the first commandment God gave to Noah after the flood (Genesis 9:6).

Plainly, the Bible distinguishes between a justified killing and murder, that is, unlawful (not legally justified) homicide in which the perpetrator intentionally kills another person. The penal codes of nations around the world have historically held a similar distinction. So God forbids murder specifically in the Ten Commandments, not killing in general.

For you fashioned my inmost being, you knit me together in my mother's womb. I thank you because I am awesomely made, wonderfully; your works are wonders – I know this very well (Psalm 139:13-14). Psalm 139 is all about the greatness of God. In verses 13-14, King David goes from speaking about God's omnipresence to speaking about God's power and skill. And the particular phase of divine omnipotence he focuses on is the marvelous development of a baby in his mother's womb. In a speck of watery material smaller than the dot over this *i*, all the future characteristics of the child are programmed – the color of his skin, eyes, and hair, the shape of his facial features, and the natural abilities he will have. All that the child will be physically and mentally is contained in germ form in that fertilized egg. From it will develop 60 trillion cells, 100 thousand miles of nerve fiber, 60 thousand miles of vessels carrying blood around the body, and 250 bones – to say nothing of joints, ligaments, and muscles. David describes the formation of the fetus with exquisite beauty.

Yes, God formed our inward parts, each one a marvel of divine engineering. Think of the brain, for instance, with its capacity for recording facts, sounds, odors, sights, touch, and pain; with its ability to recall; with its power to make computations; and with its seemingly endless flair for making decisions and solving problems. And God knit us together in our mother's womb. This aptly describes the marvelous weaving of the muscles, sinews, ligaments, nerves, blood vessels, and bones of the human frame. So David bursts forth in praise to the Lord. As he thinks of man, the crown of God's creation, he can only confess that he is fearfully and wonderfully made. The more we think of the marvels of the human body – its orderliness, its complexity, its beauty, its instincts, and its inherited factors – the more we wonder how anyone trained in natural science can fail to be a believer in an infinite Creator as well as wanting to protect that which this Creator holds sacred, namely, human life.

The more we think of the marvels of the human body the more we wonder how anyone trained in natural science can fail to be a believer.

It only seems right to protect the life of the unborn. Does the Bible make mention of the rights of the unborn? The answer is an emphatic yes! Look at Exodus 21:22-25: *"If people are fighting with each other and happen to hurt a pregnant woman so badly that her unborn child dies, then, even if no other harm follows, he must be fined. He must pay the amount set by the*

woman's husband and confirmed by judges. But if any harm fol-
lows, then you are to give life for life, eye for eye, tooth for tooth,
hand for hand, foot for foot, burn for burn, wound for wound
and bruise for bruise."

The general rule concerning personal injury was life for life, eye for eye, tooth for tooth. This teaches that in God's kingdom, the penalty should fit the crime, avoiding excessive leniency or extreme severity, for this is justice. Make no mistake; Yeshua came to bring life. *"The thief comes only in order to steal, kill and destroy; I have come so that they may have life, life in its fullest measure"* (John 10:10).

The purpose of the thief is to steal, kill, and destroy. He comes for purely selfish motives. In order to fulfill his own desires, he would even kill the sheep. But Messiah Yeshua does not come to the human heart for any selfish reason. He comes to give, not to get. He comes so that people may have life, and that they may have it more abundantly. We receive life the moment we accept Him as our Savior. After we are saved, however, we find that there are various degrees of enjoyment of this life. The more we turn ourselves over to the Holy Spirit, the more we enjoy the life that has been given to us. We not only have life at that moment, but we also have it more abundantly.

CHAPTER 6

GOD HATES A HEART THAT PLOTS WICKED SCHEMES

God hates a heart that plots wicked schemes. The word *plot* comes to us from the Hebrew word *khaw-rash*, and it means "to plough or engrave." Figuratively the word means "to devise in a bad sense." The word *scheme* is *makh-ash-aw-baw* in the Hebrew, and it means "an invention, a plan, or a purpose." Therefore, a person who plots wicked schemes is a person who is constantly inventing and masterminding vile plans. This, of course, refers to the unregenerate mind that is always plotting some kind of evil. The evil thoughts come from an evil mind. The Lord Yeshua listed some of these wicked imaginations in Mark 7:21-22 as follows: *"For from within, out of a person's heart, come forth wicked thoughts, sexual immorality, theft, murder, adultery, greed, malice, deceit, indecency, envy, slander, arrogance, foolishness."*

One who is not born again, or who has an unregenerate heart, will think these things on a regular basis. We are not talking about intermittent sin that needs to be repented of; rather, we are referring to a lifestyle of sin and wickedness. If you are truly born again, you will plot holy and righteous schemes. You will think upon things above as opposed to things below.

Colossians 3:2 says, *Focus your minds on the things above, not on things here on earth.* The believer's outlook should not be earthbound. He should view things not as they appear to the natural eye but in reference to their importance to God. A. T. Robertson said, "The baptized life means that the believer is seeking heaven and is thinking heaven. His feet are upon the earth, but his head is with the stars. He is living like a citizen of heaven here on earth." If this were the case, one would dwell on that which is good, and their ultimate desire would be to be a blessing to all and to glorify God.

There are a great many words in both the Hebrew language and the Greek language that are translated *mind*. In the Bible, the word that is often translated *mind* is the word for *heart*. It refers to the inner being of the person – the will and the seat of one's emotions. It is basically the person's decision maker. Today, we often set the mind and heart against each other as in "even though he knew in his mind it was a bad idea, he had to follow his heart." This is simply a modern invention that differentiates intellect from emotions.

In ancient times, this modern-day distinction was much less emphasized. For example, when Yeshua tells us to love the Lord with all our heart, soul, and mind, He is not highlighting various aspects of our personality, nor is He differentiating between emotion and intellect; rather, He is saying that our love for God should be all-inclusive. In other words, we should love God with the totality of our being. According to the *International Standard Bible Encyclopedia,* the mind is simply the inner being or the sum total of all our mental, emotional, and spiritual faculties without drawing fine distinctions between them.

Second Corinthians 10:5 says, *Every arrogance that raises itself up against the knowledge of God; we take every thought captive and make it obey the Messiah.* Taking every thought captive sounds like a great idea, but is it possible? Well, if we trust God's Word, then it is possible. Many human thoughts, speculations, and man-made philosophies, if entertained, can hold us in bondage. Things like the theory of evolution, secular humanism (humanity is capable of morality and self-fulfillment without belief in God), as well as the cults and false religions have created thinking that has imprisoned the minds of millions. All men's teachings and speculations must be judged in the light of the teachings of the Messiah. We must not allow our thinking to be in defiance of the Word of God.

> *All men's teachings and speculations must be judged in the light of the teachings of the Messiah.*

In conclusion, brothers, focus your thoughts on what is true, noble, righteous, pure, lovable or admirable, on some virtue or on something praiseworthy (Philippians 4:8). Here the apostle gives a closing bit of advice concerning the thought life. The Bible everywhere teaches that we can control what we think. It is useless to adopt a defeatist attitude saying that we simply cannot help it when our minds are filled with unwelcome thoughts. The fact of the matter is we *can* help it. The secret lies in the biblical definition of positive thinking.

One definition of positive thinking is "the act of renewing thought processes in order to identify areas that need improvement, and then using the appropriate tools to change those thoughts in a positive, goal-oriented way." Of course, thinking positively is not wrong. The problem associated with positive thinking is in believing that there is some kind of supernatural power in positive thinking. In this age of rampant false doctrines and watered-down theology, the power of positive thinking has stood out as one of the more popular errors.

The idea of the power of positive thinking was popularized by Dr. Norman Vincent Peale in his book *The Power of Positive Thinking* (1952). According to Peale, people can change future outcomes and events by thinking them into existence. The power of positive thinking promotes self-confidence and faith in oneself. Peale wrote, "When you expect the best, you release a magnetic force in your mind which by a law of attraction tends to bring the best to you."[4] Of course, there is nothing biblical about one's mind emanating a magnetic force that pulls good things into one's orbit. In fact, there is much that is unbiblical about such a notion.

In *The Power of Positive Thinking,* Peale used flawless religious concepts and subjective psychological theories to advance a false version of faith and hope. His theory is part of the "self-help" movement whereby a person tries to create his own reality with human effort, proper mental images, and willpower. But reality is truth, and the truth is found in the Bible. Peale's theory is flawed because he did not base it on truth.

---

4   Norman Vincent Peale, *The Power of Positive Thinking* (Hoboken, New Jersey: Prentice-Hall, 1952).

The positive thinking that the Bible is referring to in Philippians 4:8 is the expulsive power of a new affection. A person cannot entertain evil thoughts and thoughts about Messiah Yeshua at the same time. If an evil thought should come to him, he should immediately get rid of it by meditating on the person and work of Yeshua. The more enlightened psychologists and psychiatrists of the day have come to agree with the apostle Paul on this matter. They stress the dangers of negative thinking.

You do not have to look very closely to find the Lord Yeshua in Philippians 4:8. Everything that is true, noble, righteous, pure, lovable, admirable, virtuous, and praiseworthy is found in Him. Let us look at these virtues one by one. *True* means not false or unreliable, but genuine and real. *Noble* implies honorable or morally attractive. *Righteous* means just toward God and man. *Pure* would refer to the high moral character of a person's life. *Lovable* has the perception of that which is admirable or agreeable to behold or consider. *Admirable* means excellent, great, and valuable. *Virtuous* speaks of moral excellence, and *praiseworthy* is something that deserves to be commended.

Everything that is true, noble, righteous, pure, lovable, admirable, virtuous, and praiseworthy is found in Yeshua.

Philippians 4:7 says, *Then God's shalom, passing all understanding, will keep your hearts and minds safe in union with the Messiah Yeshua.* Here, Paul assured the saints that God would fortify their hearts and thoughts in Messiah Yeshua. But he is not neglectful to remind them that they, too, have a responsibility in the matter. God does not fortify the thought life of a man who does not want it to be kept pure.

We must be careful when it comes to our thinking. Proverbs 24:8-9 says, *He who plans to do evil people call a schemer. The evil plans of the foolish are sin, and people detest a scorner.* The one who uses his God-given faculties to invent new forms of evil earns the title of master schemer. The devising of foolishness is sin, and the arrogant scoffer who is brazen in his wickedness earns the contempt of others.

Proverbs 14:22 says, *Won't those who plot evil go astray? But grace and truth are for those who plan good.* Those who plot mischief and devise evil plans are destined to go astray, for God hates a heart that plots wicked schemes. But those who devise good for others are rewarded with grace and truth. This means that God shows kindness to them and is true to His promises of protection and reward. How blessed are those who bless others.

CHAPTER 7

GOD HATES FEET THAT ARE
SWIFT IN RUNNING TO DO EVIL

The reason some have *feet swift in running to do evil* is because they have *a heart that plots wicked schemes* – a person's heart will shape their actions (Proverbs 6:18-19). This is why it is so important to consider one's thinking and feelings. We see in this proverb that God not only hates the mind that plans the evil, but He hates the feet that are eager to carry it out as well. It is bad enough to dwell on evil schemes, but to carry them out is much more distasteful and warrants hatred from almighty God.

One must be very careful with their thoughts. If you think about something long and hard enough, your actions will follow suit. In most versions of the Bible, Proverbs 23:7 says, *As a man thinks, so he is.* This verse, like so many others, is not read in context and is often mistranslated and therefore misunderstood. Taken out of context, this verse is used to support self-centered, self-promoting positive thinking. So if you think of yourself as rich, you will be rich, and if you think of yourself as poor, you will be poor. As you think in your heart, so you are. Such a faulty interpretation has nothing to do with the context of Proverbs 23:7.

Proverbs 23:7 in the *Complete Jewish Bible* says, *For he is like someone who keeps accounts — "Eat! Drink!" he says to you, but he doesn't really mean it.* This passage advises against taking up an offer that is not genuinely from the heart. The point of the statement – *as a man thinks, so he is* – is that outward actions can be deceiving, but a person's heart determines what a person is really like. It's not what a man says that counts, it's what he thinks that counts.

Above everything else, guard your heart; for it is the source of life's consequences (Proverbs 4:23). The heart/mind is the fountain from which the actions spring forth. If the fountain is pure, the stream that flows from it will be pure. Our thoughts produce our actions. We have to be careful of periodicals, videos, websites, conversations, and situations that will set us up for a fall. We should also avoid spending time with those who would encourage us to go down these wrong paths. In other words, you are what you eat, and as the saying goes, "Garbage in, garbage out."

> *The heart/mind is the fountain from which the actions spring forth.*

We have to practice thought replacement. Ephesians 4:22-23 says, *Then, so far as your former way of life is concerned, you must strip off your old nature, because your old nature is thoroughly rotted by its deceptive desires; and you must let your spirits and minds keep being renewed.*

We need to do a complete about-face in our thinking, over and over again. The Spirit of God influences our thought processes to reason from God's standpoint, not from man's. We are to pursue God intensely, replacing sinful thoughts with godly pursuits and mindsets. When tempted to hate someone, we replace those hateful thoughts with godly actions: We do good to them, speak well of them, and pray for them. Merely seeking to put off sinful thoughts without replacing those thoughts with godly ones leaves an open field for satan to come along and sow his weeds.

We are citizens of heaven, so our way of life is not the same as those on earth. Yes, we are *in* this world, but not *of* this world. We are born anew, and we are being renewed in the spirit of our minds. This encompasses a complete about-face in our thinking, a change from mental impurity to holiness. The Spirit of God influences the thought processes to reason from God's standpoint, not from that of unsaved men.

First Corinthians 2:14 says, *Now the natural man does not receive the things from the Spirit of God – to him they are nonsense! Moreover, he is unable to grasp them, because they are evaluated through the Spirit.* The reason nonbelievers do not respond to biblical truth is that they cannot discern biblical truth. These truths can only be discerned by the power of the Spirit of God. Trying to explain God's program to unregenerate men is like trying to describe a sunset to a blind man, or discussing nuclear physics with a monument in the park.

Most importantly, one must be born again to get the mind of Messiah. The most important steps are sometimes rushed. The gospel is a call for the unbeliever to repent of his sin and embrace Yeshua by faith. The word *repentance* carries the notion of a change of mind; therefore, our thinking must be changed from old, ungodly ways of thinking to new, godly ways of thinking. Our thinking, or what we know in our minds to be true, forms a conviction in our hearts of that truth, and that conviction in our hearts translates into action. There are no shortcuts and no magical formulas for changing our thinking. Just as it is futile to take antibiotic after antibiotic for a recurring infection, we must attack our fruitless thinking at the fundamental level rather than wait for it to become rooted in our lives by actions and then try to pull it out.

Our thoughts have power. Thoughts in line with the Word of God will protect us, but negative thoughts will cost us dearly.

Thoughts in line with the Word of God will protect us, but negative thoughts will cost us dearly.

Thoughts can come into our minds from all sides, but we can choose what will stay and what we will cast out. According to medical science, toxic thoughts, such as stress, worry, fear, anger, and unforgiveness, actually cause damage to the brain. Chemicals are released into the brain, causing chaos and damage. In a spiritual sense, those toxic thoughts connect us to the curse. When we renew our minds to the fact that thoughts matter, we begin to detoxify our brains and switch over from fear, worry, and anger to power, love, and a sound mind. We have to be intentional about being intentional.

Not only do we need to be extremely careful regarding our thought life, but we also have to be careful about our surroundings, as we tend to become products of our environment. We have to keep in mind that Lot made a crucial mistake in his life when he set his tent towards Sodom:

> *Lot, who was traveling with Avram, also had flocks, herds and tents. But the land could not support their living together, because their possessions were too great for them to remain together. Moreover, quarreling arose between Avram's and Lot's herdsmen. The Kena'ani and the P'rizi were then living in the land. Avram said to Lot, "Please, let's not have quarreling between me and you, or between my herdsmen and yours, since we're kinsmen. Isn't the whole land there in front of you? Please separate yourself from me – if you go to the left, I will go to the right; if you go to the right, I will go to the left." Lot looked up and saw that the whole plain of the Yarden was well watered everywhere, before ADONAI destroyed S'dom and 'Amora, like the garden of ADONAI, like the land of Egypt in the direction of Tzo'ar. So Lot chose all the plain of the Yarden for himself, and Lot traveled eastward; thus they separated themselves from each other. Avram lived in the land of Kena'an; and Lot lived in the cities of the plain, setting up his tent near S'dom. Now the men of S'dom were evil, committing great sins against ADONAI.* (Genesis 13:5-13)

The herdsmen of Lot and Abram quarreled over pastureland for their flocks. In true courtesy, kindness, and unselfishness, Abram offered Lot his choice of all the land. Lot chose the lush pastures of the Jordan Valley, adjacent to the sin cities of Sodom and Gomorrah. Lot was a true believer, as it says in 2 Peter 2:7-8: *He rescued Lot, a righteous man who was distressed by the debauchery of those unprincipled people; for the wicked deeds which that righteous man saw and heard, as he lived among them, tormented his righteous heart day after day.*

However, Lot was a world borderer. The fact that the men of Sodom were exceedingly wicked and sinful against the Lord did not restrain Lot in his choice. Notice the steps in his plunge into worldliness: He (his men) experienced strife (Genesis 13:7); he saw (13:10); he chose (13:11); and he pitched his tent toward (13:12). Following the story, Lot resided away from the place where God's priest was (Genesis 14:12); and he sat in the gate, the place of political power (Genesis 19:1). He became a local official in Sodom.

He saw, he chose, he became. Many years ago, there was what was called "the dessert cart" displayed at restaurants. At the end of the meal, the server would literally wheel over to the table a cart of all types of different desserts that the restaurant had to offer. They would display them in a delectable array. The theory behind the dessert cart is that once a patron saw the desserts, he would be hard-pressed not to want one. An old adage says, "Just because I'm on a diet doesn't mean I can't look at the menu." I believe that if you look long and hard enough at the menu, diet or no diet, you might just put in your order.

Proverbs 1:15-16 says, *My son, don't go along with them, don't set foot on their path; their feet run to evil, they rush to shed blood.* The voice of wisdom cries out, "My son, don't do it. Stay as far away from them as possible. Have nothing to do with their plans. Run away!"

.

CHAPTER 8

GOD HATES A FALSE WITNESS
WHO LIES WITH EVERY BREATH

[God hates] a false witness who lies with every breath. (Proverbs 6:19)

A false witness will not go unpunished; whoever breathes out lies will not escape. (Proverbs 19:5)

A false witness will not go unpunished; whoever breathes out lies will perish. (Proverbs 19:9)

A lying witness is doomed, but one who heard [what was said] will testify successfully. (Proverbs 21:28)

We should not be surprised at the frequency with which this is repeated. After all, one of the Ten Commandments deals with perjury. Bearing false witness is mentioned many times in the Bible, exclusively as something bad. *"You shall not bear false witness against your neighbor"* is the ninth of the Ten Commandments that Moses brought back with him from his encounter with God on Mount Sinai (Exodus 20:16 ESV).

A false witness, or one who spreads a false report, is associated with being allied with the wicked (Exodus 23:1), willing to do violence to others (Psalm 27:12), and sowing discord among brothers (Proverbs 6:19).

The Bible calls bearing false witness *lying*. Proverbs 14:5 says, *An honest witness will not lie, but a false witness lies with every breath*. It is better to go to heaven with a good conscience than to stay on earth with a bad one. How careful we should be to be utterly truthful at all times!

Proverbs 25:18 says, *Like a club, a sword or a sharp arrow is a person who gives false testimony against a neighbor*. The

> *The proverb compares a man who bears false witness against his neighbor to a violent weapon.*

proverb compares a man who bears false witness against his neighbor to a violent weapon. We see three apt similes for the man who bears false witness against his neighbor: a club, which is used for mauling and smashing to pieces; a sword, with its two sharp edges used for cutting and killing; and a sharp arrow, used for piercing and wounding.

Lies harm people. A false witness is one who stands up and swears before others that something untrue is true, especially with the intention of hurting someone or ruining their reputation. This happened to David (Psalm 27:12), Stephen (Acts 6:13), and Yeshua (Matthew 26:60; Mark 14:56).

When the wicked Queen Jezebel wished to procure a vineyard for her sulking husband, King Ahab, she employed two false witnesses. Naboth, the rightful owner of the vineyard, was seated in an honorable place on a day of fasting, but *the two good-for-nothing men came in and sat opposite him, and these scoundrels publicly accused Navot, saying, "Navot cursed God and the king." So they took him outside the city and stoned him to death* (1 Kings 21:13).

What the *scoundrels* said against Navot (Naboth) was absolutely untrue; they were bearing false witness with exemption from punishment and with the queen's blessing. The treacherous Jezebel thus framed Naboth so that it would appear he was being executed for breaking the law of God. As a result, an innocent man was killed. When a person is righteous and his enemies can find nothing with which to blame him, bearing false witness is a common weapon.

The lies told by a false witness come from the sinful human heart – along with murder, adultery, sexual immorality, theft, slander, and evil thoughts (Matthew 15:19). Yeshua said that man is defiled by these evil things that come from the heart. The only possible cure for an evil heart that bears false witness is to receive a new, pure heart, which can only be given by God (Ezekiel 36:26). When a person is indwelt by the Holy Spirit, he will be like a fresh spring or a fruitful tree or a budding vine, bursting with good things (John 7:38; Psalm 1:1-6; John 15:4-5). The old is gone, and the new takes its place: *So far as your former way of life is concerned, you must strip off your old nature, because your old nature is thoroughly rotted by its deceptive desires; and you must let your spirits and minds keep being renewed, and clothe yourselves with the new nature created to be godly, which expresses itself in the righteousness and holiness that flow from the truth* (Ephesians 4:22-24).

The *old* means all that he was before his conversion, all that he was as a child of Adam. The old is corrupted due to giving in to deceitful evil cravings of the old heart. What was once pleasant and promising is now hideous and disappointing. The renewal is accomplished by the Spirit of God. The Spirit influences our new nature, and we carry out its orders. We put on the new man, the new heart, and right conduct toward others, and piety toward God is the result. What we need to do is to attend the funeral of our old self daily.

Those who are in Messiah have a new heart that speaks the truth. Ephesians 4:25 says, *Therefore, stripping off falsehood, let everyone speak truth with his neighbor, because we are intimately related to each other as parts of a body.* Paul says that because believers have put off the old man and have put on the new man through their union with Messiah, they should demonstrate this startling reversal in their everyday lives. They can do this by putting away lying and putting on truthfulness. Lying here includes every form of dishonesty, whether it is shading of the truth, exaggeration, cheating, failure to keep promises, betrayal of confidence, flattery, or fudging on income taxes. The believer's word should be absolutely trustworthy. His yes should mean yes and his no should mean no. The life of a believer becomes a libel rather than a Bible when he stoops to any form of tampering with truthfulness.

Truth is a debt we owe to all men. However, when Paul uses the word *neighbor* here, he is thinking particularly of our fellow believers. This is clear from the motive given: for we are members of one another (cf. Romans 12:5; 1 Corinthians 12:12-27). It is as unthinkable for one believer to lie to another as it would be for a nerve in the body to deliberately send a false message to the brain, or for the eye to deceive the rest of the body when danger is approaching.

A person who bears false witness is controlled by the flesh rather than by the Spirit of God, and he should repent of that sin and turn to Yeshua. In Proverbs 6:19, it is a matter of public testimony in a court of law. In Proverbs 6:17, it was more a matter of everyday conversation.

Exodus 23:1-3 says, *"You are not to repeat false rumors; do not join hands with the wicked by offering perjured testimony. Do not follow the crowd when it does what is wrong; and don't allow the popular view to sway you into offering testimony for any cause if the effect will be to pervert justice. On the other hand, don't favor a person's lawsuit simply because he is poor."*

> It is as unthinkable for one believer to lie to another as it would be for a nerve in the body to deliberately send a false message to the brain.

In judicial matters the children of God were forbidden to circulate a false report, to conspire with the wicked to defend the guilty, to take sides with an evil crowd, or to show partiality to the poor.

Proverbs 12:17 says, *He who tells the truth furthers justice, but a false witness furthers deceit.* A witness who tells the truth in court gives righteous evidence. A false witness tells lies. We are asked the following question in a court of law: "Do you swear or affirm, under penalty of perjury, that the testimony you're about to give is the truth, the whole truth, and nothing but the truth, so help you God?" I can only imagine how differently some verdicts would go if more people believed in and feared the Lord. For that matter, the whole entire spiritual climate of the universe would change for the better. There was a time when the fear of the Lord was alive and well in our nation, and the thought of falling into the hands of the living God was a fearful thing.

There once was a little boy who had a very bad habit of lying about others. His father decided to hand him a bag of nails and said that every time the boy lied, he had to hammer a nail into the fence.

On the first day, the boy hammered twenty-seven nails into that fence.

The boy gradually began to control his lying over the next few weeks, and the number of nails he was hammering into the fence slowly decreased. He discovered it was easier to control his tongue than to hammer those nails into the fence. Finally, the day came when the boy didn't lie at all. He told his father the news, and the father suggested that the boy should now pull out a nail every day he kept his tongue from lying.

The days passed and the young boy was finally able to tell his father that all the nails were gone. The father took his son by the hand and led him to the fence.

"You have done well, my son, but look at the holes in the fence. The fence will never be the same. When you tell lies about another, they leave a scar just like this one. You can put a knife in a man and draw it out. It won't matter how many times you say, 'I'm sorry,' the wound is still there."[5]

"Do not give false evidence against your neighbor" (Exodus 20:16). This commandment, which is repeated over

---

5   Teachnet Staff, Adapted from "Story: The Fence," *Teachnet*, November 7, 2010. *Teachnet: www.teachnet.com/communicate/inspiration/story-the-fence/* (August 2022).

and over again in the Scriptures, forbids making statements about another person that are not true. Why is this so worthy of repetition? Because when we give false evidence against our neighbor, we can damage the person's character, even possibly causing him to be punished or, worse yet, even executed. It is so sad to think of all the people whose lives were ruined

When we give false evidence against our neighbor, we can damage the person's character.

because of false testimony. We must have respect and concern for another's reputation so much so that we will not ever bear false witness!

CHAPTER 9

GOD HATES ONE WHO SOWS DISCORD AMONG BRETHREN

The striking thing here is that God ranks the one who causes divisions among brethren with murderers, liars, and perjurers. We, in the body of Messiah, tend to rank which sins we consider detestable and which sins we consider minor offenses towards God. What we need to do is to take God at His word and agree with it all.

Divisions can lead to all kinds of evil, and this is why they are so detestable to God. In addition to this is the fact that the God of the Bible is a unified plurality, or a plural unity. God said from the very beginning that the two shall become one flesh (Genesis 2:24). The adversary, on the other hand, does all in his power to make the one flesh two. It is his modus operandi to divide and conquer. Yeshua Himself says, *"If a kingdom is divided against itself, that kingdom can't survive; and if a household is divided against itself, that household can't survive"* (Mark 3:24-25). Continued survival depends upon internal cooperation, not antagonism. So when we cause divisions, we are playing into satan's hands, and God hates it!

Romans 12:18 says, *If possible, and to the extent that it depends on you, live in peace with all people.* Believers should not be needlessly irritating or quarrelsome. The righteousness of God is not worked out by aggressiveness and rage. We should love peace, make peace, and be at peace.

It was the Messiah Himself that said, *"How blessed are those who make peace! for they will be called sons of God"* (Matthew 5:9). Notice that the Lord is not speaking about people with a peaceful disposition or those who love peace. He is referring to those who actively intervene to make peace.

The natural approach is to watch strife from the sidelines. The divine approach is to take positive action toward creating peace, even if it means receiving insults and abuse. Peacemakers are called sons of God. This is not how they become sons of God; that can only happen by receiving Yeshua as Messiah (John 1:12). By making peace, believers manifest themselves as sons of God, and God will one day acknowledge them as people who bear the family likeness. We are called to sow the seeds of the kingdom, and unity and harmony are those seeds.

We are called to sow the seeds of the kingdom, and unity and harmony are those seeds.

In Galatians 6:7, Paul reminds readers – *Don't delude yourselves: no one makes a fool of God! A person reaps what he sows.*

God is a just God and has instituted throughout human experience the concept of sowing and reaping. When a farmer plants seeds and cares for those seeds, they will usually sprout and produce growth. In the same way, whatever a person "plants" in his own thinking and behavior will later bear fruit – either good or bad. If a person is focused on fulfilling the desires of the flesh, and that is what he invests in, then that person will reap fruit from that investment. Paul describes this fruit in Galatians 5:19-21, and the list is not pretty. On the other hand, if one invests in spiritual things, then the "fruit" in his life will be spiritual and wholesome (Galatians 6:8). Paul explains how the Holy Spirit produces fruit in people and what it looks like (Galatians 5:22-23).

With a somber warning Paul introduces the truth that what a man sows he also reaps: *Do not be deceived: God is not mocked* (Galatians 6:7 ESV). Wise readers will take heed to their own lives and take steps to ensure they live according to this principle. Let no one entertain the idea that he or she is the exception to the rule. Reaping follows sowing, and it matters what you sow. God searches the heart and knows every circumstance, and His decree that the harvest will match the planting will not be set aside.

Paul further explains elsewhere the concept that whatever a man sows he also reaps. In 1 Corinthians 3:8, he asserts that each person will be rewarded according to his or her own work. Neither the one who plants nor the one who waters are the most significant factor in the equation, because God causes the growth, *So neither the planter nor the waterer is anything, only God who makes things grow – planter and waterer are the same. However, each will be rewarded according to his work* (1 Corinthians 3:7-8). Even when we are planting and watering well, focusing on the things related to our new life in Messiah, it is still God who causes the growth. And even though God rewards the one who works, we understand that even our opportunity to work is a gift from God. In other words, the principle that whatever a man sows he also reaps teaches both God's justice and His mercy.

The word *discord* is synonymous with disharmony, divisions, tumult, disagreements, and strife. There are those who love to sow discord. It's almost as if they are being subsidized by the government to do so. A close cousin to sowing discord is gossip.

Proverbs 26:20-21 says, *If there's no wood, the fire goes out; if nobody gossips, contention stops. As coals are to embers and wood to fire is a quarrelsome person to kindling strife.* Just as fuel feeds a fire, so gossip feeds trouble. Unless a troublemaker keeps adding aggravations, gossip, and lies, strife will soon die out. Some years ago, the following appeared in the *Atlanta Journal:* "I am more deadly than the screaming shell of a howitzer. I win without killing. I tear down homes, break hearts, and wreck lives. I travel on the wings of the wind. No innocence is strong enough to daunt me, I have no regard for truth, no respect for justice, no mercy for the defenseless. My victims are as numerous as the sands on the sea and often as innocent. I never forget and seldom forgive. My name is Gossip!"

In other words, we absolutely must be careful in regards to what we sow.

We can apply the principle of reaping what we sow to the matter of salvation. If we do not know Messiah Yeshua as our

Savior, then we are still dead in our sins or separated from having a right relationship with God:

> *You used to be dead because of your sins and acts of disobedience. You walked in the ways of the 'olam hazeh* [the present world] *and obeyed the Ruler of the Powers of the Air, who is still at work among the disobedient. Indeed, we all once lived this way – we followed the passions of our old nature and obeyed the wishes of our old nature and our own thoughts. In our natural condition we were headed for God's wrath, just like everyone else. But God is so rich in mercy and loves us with such intense love that, even when we were dead because of our acts of disobedience, he brought us to life along with the Messiah – it is by grace that you have been delivered.* (Ephesians 2:1-5)

If we are in that state, even our righteous deeds are as unclean rags in comparison with God's standard of righteousness (Isaiah 64:6). If we are in that condition, the truth that whatever a man sows he also reaps (Galatians 6:7) is actually terrifying because we are sowing according to sin and death, and the fruit will reflect that. On the other hand, if in His infinite mercy God has made us alive together with Messiah by grace through faith (Ephesians 2:8-10), then we have the opportunity to sow

If in His infinite mercy God has made us alive by grace through faith, then we have the opportunity to sow according to newness of life.

according to newness of life. Because of His grace we can now invest in things that have eternal value and see fruit that also has eternal value.

The fact that whatever a man sows he also reaps is not only about justice, but also about God's magnificent mercy. God hasn't given us what we deserved; in His amazing grace God has given us what we did not deserve – the opportunity to sow the seed of righteousness so that we can see the fruit of His righteousness in our lives.

J. A. Froude, the historian, said, "One lesson, and only one, history may be said to repeat distinctness that the world is built on moral foundations, that in the long run, it is well with the good, and in the long run it is ill with the wicked."[6]

---

6   James Anthony Froude, "The Science of History," in *Short Studies on Great Subjects* (New York: Scribner, Armstrong & Co., 1873), 22.

CHAPTER 10

GOD LOVES MANKIND

John 3:16 says, *For God loved the world in this way: He gave his one and only Son, so that everyone who believes in him will not perish but have eternal life.*[7]

This is one of the best-known verses in the Bible, doubtless because it states the gospel so clearly and succinctly. It summarizes what Messiah Yeshua had been teaching Nakdimon (Nicodemus) concerning the manner by which the new birth is received. *God*, we read, *loved the world. The world* here includes all mankind. God does not love men's sins or the wicked world system, but He extended His love towards people and is not willing that any should perish (2 Peter 3:9).

The extent of His love is shown by the fact that He gave His only begotten Son. God has no other Son like Messiah Yeshua. It was an expression of His infinite love that He would be willing

---

7   From the Christian Standard Bible

to give His unique Son for a race of rebel sinners. This does not mean that everyone is saved (a false teaching known as "universal salvation"). A person must receive what Messiah has done for him before God will give him eternal life. Therefore, these words are added: *so that everyone who believes in him will not perish but have eternal life.* There is no need for anyone to perish. A way has been provided by which all might be saved, but a person must acknowledge Yeshua as their personal Savior. When they do this, they have eternal life as a present possession. F. W. Boreham says, "When the body of Messiah comes to understand the love with which God loved the world, she will be restless and ill at ease until all the great empires have been captured, until every coral island has been won."[8]

With that great truth being said, if we are going to love that which God loves, then first we need to love the world too! The idea here is to emulate God. We are called to be God's imitators, not His impersonators.

Ephesians 5:1-2 says, *So imitate God, as his dear children; and live a life of love, just as also the Messiah loved us, indeed, on our behalf gave himself up as an offering, as a slaughtered sacrifice to God with a pleasing fragrance.* The last verse in Ephesians chapter 4 actually connects to the first verse in Ephesians chapter 5. Ephesians 4:32 says, *Instead, be kind to each other, tenderhearted; and forgive each other, just as in the Messiah God has also forgiven you.* Kindness is an unselfish concern for the welfare of others and a desire to be helpful even at great personal sacrifice. Tenderheartedness is a sympathetic, affectionate, and compassionate interest in others and

---

8   Frank W. Boreham, *Mountains in the Mist: Some Australian Reveries* (New York: Abingdon Press, 1919), 20.

a willingness to bear their burden. And of course, forgiveness is a readiness to pardon offenses, to overlook personal wrongs against oneself, and to harbor no desire for retaliation.

The greatest example of One who forgives is God Himself. The basis of His forgiveness is the work of Yeshua at Golgotha. And we are the unworthy objects. God could not forgive sin without proper satisfaction, which His righteousness demanded. In Messiah Yeshua, in His person and work, God found a righteous basis on which He could forgive us. Since He forgave us when we were in debt for millions of dollars, we ought to forgive others when they owe us a few dollars (Matthew 18:23-28).

In Messiah Yeshua, in His person and work, God found a righteous basis on which He could forgive us.

God's example of forgiveness in Ephesians 4:32 forms the basis of Paul's exhortation here in Ephesians 5:1. The connection is this: God in Messiah has forgiven you. Now be imitators of God in forgiving one another. The word *imitate* is originally from the Greek word *mim-ay-tace,* which is where we get the word *mimic* in the English language, meaning "to copy in action." In short, it means "to follow," which is the basic definition of a follower. This is why Yeshua spoke to the original twelve disciples and said, *"Follow me"* (Matthew 4:19; Mark 2:14; Luke 5:27; John 1:43).

Another way in which we should resemble the Lord is by walking in love: *live a life of love, just as also the Messiah loved us, indeed, on our behalf gave himself up as an offering, as a slaughtered sacrifice to God with a pleasing fragrance* (Ephesians 5:2). The rest of the verse explains that to walk in love means to give ourselves for others. That is what Yeshua, our perfect example did. Amazing fact! He loves us. The proof of His love is that He gave Himself for us in death at Golgotha. The Lord Yeshua pleased His Father by giving Himself for others. The moral of the story is that we too can bring joy to God by giving ourselves for others.

The apostle Paul also said in 1 Corinthians 11:1, *Try to imitate me, even as I myself try to imitate the Messiah*. Paul had been speaking in the previous chapter of how he tried to gauge all his actions in light of their effect on others. Now he tells the Corinthians to imitate him, just as he also imitated Yeshua. He renounced personal advantages and rights in order to help those around him. He told the Corinthians to do likewise and not selfishly parade their freedoms in such a way as to hinder the gospel of Messiah or offend the weak brother.

We are well aware that Yeshua is the one and only unique Son of God. He is the only way to the Father (John 14:6). He is also the perfect role model to demonstrate what a son of God should look like in word and deed, as opposed to any external physical attributes. It is important to study His life and do all we can through the magnificent power of the Holy Spirit to emulate Him.

Many today want to have role models to look up to or people they aspire to be like. We in the body of Messiah have but one role model, and His name is Yeshua. Yeshua said, *"Take my yoke upon you and learn from me, because I am gentle and humble in heart, and you will find rest for your souls"* (Matthew 11:29). To take his yoke upon us is to enter into submission to His will, to turn over control of our life to Him. To learn from Him means that as we acknowledge His lordship in every area of our lives, He thereby trains us in His ways. For He is gentle and lowly in heart, which was in stark contrast to the Pharisees who were harsh and proud. As the true Teacher of God, Yeshua is meek and lowly. Those who take His yoke will learn to take the lowest place, and esteem others more than themselves. *Do nothing out of rivalry or vanity; but, in humility, regard each other as better than yourselves* (Philippians 2:3). To esteem others better than ourselves is utterly foreign to the human mind, and we cannot do it in our own strength. It is only as we are indwelt and empowered by the Holy Spirit that we can put it into practice.

God really does love the world, and He proved it! Yeshua said, *"This is my command: that you keep on loving each other just as I have loved you. No one has greater love than a person who lays down his life for his friends"* (John 15:12-13). The Lord would soon leave His disciples. They would be left in a hostile world. As tensions increased, there would be the danger of the disciples contending with one another. So the Lord leaves this standing order: *"Keep on loving each other just as I have loved you."* He told them their love should be of such a nature that they would be willing to die for one another.

People who are willing to do this do not fight with each other. The greatest example of human self-sacrifice was a man willing to die for his friends. The disciples of Messiah are called to this type of devotion. Some lay down their lives in a literal sense; others spend their whole lives in untiring service for the people of God. Messiah Yeshua is the perfect example. He laid down His life for His friends. Of course, they were enemies when He died for them, but when they were saved, they became

His friends. So it is correct to say that He died for His friends as well as for His enemies.

We are to love the world just as our Lord loves the world – with no exceptions. When the Bible speaks to us about not loving the world, it is referring to the world system that man has built in order to make himself happy without God – a kingdom that is antagonistic to God. The god and prince of this world is satan (2 Corinthians 4:4; John 12:31; 14:30; 16:11). All unsaved people are his subjects. He has succeeded in putting a veil over the minds of the unbelieving ones. He would keep them in perpetual darkness, if not for the light of the gospel of the glory of Messiah shining on them that they might be saved.

In our physical universe, the sun is always shining. We do not always see it, because sometimes something comes between the sun and us. So it is with the gospel. The light of the gospel is always shining. God is always seeking to shine into the hearts of men, but a cloud of pride, or of rebellion, or of self-righteousness, or a myriad of other things may serve effectively to hinder the light of the gospel. Satan simply does not want men to be saved.

The light of the gospel is always shining, but a cloud of pride or of self-righteousness, may hinder the light.

He seeks to attract and hold people through the lust of the flesh (sensual bodily appetites that proceed from within our evil nature), the lust of the eyes (evil desires that may arise from what we see), and the pride of life (an unholy ambition for self-display and self-glory), *because all the things of the world – the desires of the old nature, the desires of the eyes, and the pretensions of life – are not from the Father but from the world*

(1 John 2:16). Satan used his cunning ways to deceive Eve with all three of these aforementioned tools. The tree was good for food – lust of the flesh. The tree was pleasant to look at – lust of the eyes. And lastly, the tree was desired to make one wise, and this describes the pride of life. Satan is using the same three elements on men today, as there is nothing new under the sun (Ecclesiastes 1:9).

We must be careful about falling prey to the world. Remember, we are in this world but not of this world: *"I have given them your word, and the world hated them, because they do not belong to the world – just as I myself do not belong to the world. I don't ask you to take them out of the world, but to protect them from the evil one. They do not belong to the world, just as I do not belong to the world"* (John 17:14-16).

The world has its own politics, art, music, religion, amusements, thought patterns, and lifestyles, and it seeks to get everyone to conform to its culture and customs. It hates non-conformists like Yeshua and His followers.

The call is not to love or be a part of the world system, but at the same time absolutely, positively, and unequivocally extend Christ's love to everyone and anyone who is part of that system. We often attempt to evangelize, but wonder why we don't get any positive results. We try to evangelize with our heads as opposed to our hearts. We will not become winners of souls until we become weepers of souls. We also want instant gratification, but we have to invest ourselves and be willing to do whatever it takes. What has happened to the body of Messiah? She no longer has the sacrificial, selfless love for the lost that the Lord had for her. Did we forget that we too were once sons of the devil, headed for perdition with our only inheritance being judgment and eternal damnation? If we're going to love what God loves, then we need to love all people too. God extended love to the world, and so should we, with no exceptions.

CHAPTER 11

GOD LOVES SINNERS

For while we were still helpless, at the right time, the Messiah died on behalf of ungodly people. Now it is a rare event when someone gives up his life even for the sake of somebody righteous, although possibly for a truly good person one might have the courage to die. But God demonstrates his own love for us in that the Messiah died on our behalf while we were still sinners. (Romans 5:6-8)

We are reminded that we were weak, helpless, without strength, and unable to save ourselves. But at the predetermined time, Messiah Yeshua visited our planet and died for men. And He did not die for good men, as some might suppose, but for the ungodly. There was no virtue and no excellence in us to commend us to God. We were utterly unworthy, but Yeshua died for us anyway.

This act of divine love was unique and unparalleled by anything in human experience. The average man's life is precious to him, and he would not think of throwing it away for an unworthy person. For example, he would not die for a murderer, an adulterer, or a mobster. In fact, he would be reluctant to die even for a righteous man, one who is honest and dependable but not especially warmhearted. It is possible, in an extreme case, that he would die for a good man, meaning one who is kind, friendly, loving, and lovable.

> *Messiah Yeshua proved Himself to be the ultimate Hero by dying to save His enemies.*

Someone who is willing to sacrifice his own life to save another person is considered a hero. But who would be willing to die for an enemy? Messiah Yeshua proved Himself to be the ultimate Hero by dying to save His enemies.

Romans 5:10 says, *For if we were reconciled with God through his Son's death when we were enemies, how much more will we be delivered by his life, now that we are reconciled!* Before a person receives salvation in Yeshua, he is considered a sinner and an enemy of God. The Bible defines a sinner as one who falls short of God's standard or one who misses the mark. Instead of loving God as Creator and Father, the sinner rebels against Him. With a sinful nature, the ungodly person is hostile toward God.

We were hostile toward the Lord and quite content to have it so. Left to ourselves, we felt no need of being reconciled to Him. The mindset of the flesh is death because it is at enmity against God. The sinner is a rebel against God and in active hostility toward Him. If any proof were needed, it is seen in the crucifixion of Messiah Yeshua. The mind of the flesh is not subject to the law of God. It wants its own will, not God's will. It wants to be its own master, not bow to His rule. Its nature is such that it cannot be subject to God's law. It is not only the inclination that is missing but the power as well. The flesh is dead toward God. Think about it – enemies of God.

As sinners, we were like prisoners bound in chains, strapped to the guillotine, and guilty as charged. We were God's enemies, about to be put to death, when Messiah Yeshua stepped in to die in our place. By this act of sending His Son to die for us, God proved how much He loved us. While we were still sinners, Yeshua died for us.

God did not share our attitude in the matter; instead He intervened in a display of pure grace. The substitutionary death of Yeshua removed the cause of our hostility toward God, namely, our sins. By faith in Messiah, we have been reconciled to God. It's as if a car was speeding directly towards us, and Yeshua not only pushed us out of the way of the speeding car, but He also got in the way of it and took the hit.

Many people miss the truth implied by the fact that Yeshua died for us *while we were still sinners.* The chronology is important. Messiah did not wait for us to clean up our act; He sacrificed Himself while we were still actively opposed to Him. Salvation does not depend on our meeting God halfway, keeping the commandments, or trying to be as good as we can. No, God completed the work of our salvation while we were in a state of open rebellion against Him. That's grace.

If God purchased our reconciliation so dearly, will He ever let us go? If we were reconciled through the death of His Son, which is a symbol of utter weakness, shall we not be preserved to the end by the present life of Messiah at the right hand of God, a life of infinite power? If His death had such a power to save us, how much more will His life have power to keep us!

The essence of God's love is apprehended in His giving: *"For God so loved the world, that he gave his only Son, that whoever believes in him should not perish but have eternal life"* (John 3:16 ESV). Elsewhere, John says, *This is real love—not that we loved God, but that he loved us and sent his Son as a sacrifice to take away our sins* (1 John 4:10 NLT). And Paul affirms that the Son of God *loved me and gave himself for me* (Galatians 2:20 NLT).

God's love was not shown to us because we first loved Him. We did not; in fact, we were His enemies and we hated Him. In other words, He did not love us because we loved Him, but He loved us in spite of our bitter antagonism toward Him. And how did He show His love? By sending His Son as the satisfaction for our sins.

The love of God in Messiah Yeshua is unprecedented. No other love has ever been more costly to its giver and less deserving to its recipient. When God the Father gave His Son Yeshua to die for us while we were still sinners, He gave everything – His own self – to rescue those who deserved nothing but judgment from Him. In giving His Son, God gave Himself, the costliest gift of all. He paid the supreme price so that we might receive the greatest love.

The love of God is completely supernatural and otherworldly.

He demonstrates His marvelous love toward us by sending His beloved Son to die for us while we were still sinners. If we ask why he did it, we must look for the answer in the sovereign will of God Himself. There was no good in us to call forth such love, but God wants none to perish and all to come to everlasting life: *The Lord is not slow in keeping his promise, as some people think of slowness; on the contrary, he is patient with you; for it is not his purpose that anyone should be destroyed, but that everyone should turn from his sins* (2 Peter 3:9).

His desire is that all should come to repentance, so He has purposely extended the time of grace so that men might have every opportunity to be saved. I can only imagine what it would look like if the body of Messiah loved sinners the way God does. There is a plethora of theology out there, and it has its merits, but what if we simply and truly followed Yeshua in obeying the greatest commandment of them all?

There was no good in us to call forth such love, but God wants none to perish and all to come to everlasting life.

When the Pharisees heard that Yeshua silenced their antagonists, the Sadducees, they came to him for an interview. Their spokesman, a lawyer, asked Yeshua to single out the greatest commandment. *"Rabbi, which of the mitzvot* [commandments] *in the Torah is the most important?"* (Matthew 22:36).

In a masterful way Messiah Yeshua summarized man's obligation to God as the first and greatest commandment. *He told him, "'You are to love ADONAI your God with all your heart and with all your soul and with all your strength.' This is the greatest and most important mitzvah"* (Matthew 22:37-38). This means that man's first obligation is to love God with the totality of his being. The heart speaks of the emotional nature; the soul speaks of the volitional nature; and the strength speaks of the physical nature. God wants all of us.

Then Yeshua added that man's second responsibility is to love his neighbor as himself. *"And a second is similar to it, 'You are to love your neighbor as yourself.' All of the Torah and the Prophets are dependent on these two mitzvot"* (Matthew 22:39-40). Albert Barnes says, "Love to God and man comprehends the whole of religion: and to produce this has been the design of Moses, the prophets, the Savior, and the apostles."[9] We should frequently ponder the words, *love your neighbor as yourself.* We should think of how much we love ourselves and how much of our activity centers on the care and comfort of ourselves. Then we should try to imagine what would happen if we showered that love on our neighbors. Then we should do it. Such behavior is not natural, it's supernatural. Only those who have been born again can do it, and then and only then by allowing Messiah to do it through them.

We can't just pray and help the homeless, and at the same time not pray and help the wicked. If we're going to love what God loves, then we need to have Christlike love for those who do wrong too. As the saying goes, "We don't have to love the sin, but we must love the sinner." Proverbs 10:12 says, *Hate stirs up disputes, but love covers all kinds of transgressions.* This should not be taken as a doctrinal explanation of how sins are put away. The guilt and penalty of sins can only be removed by the blood of Messiah. Neither should the statement be used to condone sin to relieve an assembly from its responsibility to discipline an offender. A hateful spirit isn't satisfied with

9   Albert Barnes, *Notes on the Bible* (1834).

forgiving and forgetting; it insists on raking up old grudges and quarrels. A heart of love draws a curtain of secrecy over the faults and failures of others. These faults and failures must be confessed and forsaken, but love does not gossip about them or keep the pot boiling.

> *I may speak in the tongues of men, even angels; but if I lack love, I have become merely blaring brass or a cymbal clanging. I may have the gift of prophecy, I may fathom all mysteries, know all things, have all faith – enough to move mountains; but if I lack love, I am nothing. I may give away everything that I own, I may even hand over my body to be burned; but if I lack love, I gain nothing. Love is patient and kind, not jealous, not boastful, not proud, rude or selfish, not easily angered, and it keeps no record of wrongs. Love does not gloat over other people's sins but takes its delight in the truth. Love always bears up, always trusts, always hopes, always endures.*
> (1 Corinthians 13:1-7)

The expression, *Love always bears up,* may mean that love patiently endures all things or that it hides or conceals the faults of others. The word *bears* may be also translated *covers.* Love does not needlessly publicize the failures of others, though it must be firm in giving godly discipline when necessary. Love always trusts; that is, it tries to put the

A heart of love draws a curtain of secrecy over the faults and failures of others.

best possible construction on actions and events. Love always hopes in the sense that it earnestly desires that all things work out for the best. Love always endures in the way of persecution or ill treatment.

Romans 2:4 says, *Or perhaps you despise the riches of his kindness, forbearance and patience; because you don't realize that God's kindness is intended to lead you to turn from your sins.* In context, Paul is speaking about the fact that God's judgment is sometimes delayed. This delay is evidence of His kindness, forbearance, and patience. His kindness speaks that He is kindly disposed to sinners, but not their sins. His forbearance describes His holding back punishment on man's wickedness and rebellion. His patience is His amazing self-restraint in spite of man's ceaseless insults. The kindness of God, as seen in His providence, protection, and preservation, is aimed at leading men to repentance. He is not willing that any should perish, but that all should come to repentance. If this is the heart of God, then this should be the heart of every believer as well.

Romans 12:9 says, *Don't let love be a mere outward show. Recoil from what is evil, and cling to what is good.* In the rest of this chapter, Paul lists some characteristics that every believer should develop when dealing with the unconverted. Love should be without hypocrisy. It should not wear a mask, but should be genuine, sincere, and unaffected. People today are more untrusting and more skittish than ever before. Our love must be real, for most people can see right through the insincere and the counterfeit. People are looking for love; however, they are looking for love in all the wrong places. Let them find Yeshua's love in you!

CHAPTER 12

GOD LOVES HIS CHILDREN

First John 3:1 says, *See what love the Father has lavished on us in letting us be called God's children! For that is what we are. The reason the world does not know us is that it has not known him.*

The thought of being born of God arrests John with wonder, and he calls on his readers to take a look at the wonderful love that brought us into the family of God. Love could have saved us without making us children of God. But the manner of God's love is shown in that He brought us into His family as children.

God extends His love to the world (John 3:16), and to sinners (Romans 5:8). Being children of God means we have been born into God's family. We become children of God through faith in Messiah Yeshua, which results in spiritual rebirth. *But to as many as did receive him, to those who put their trust in his person and power, he gave the right to become children of God, not because of bloodline, physical impulse or human intention, but because of God* (John 1:12-13). God's children have a special place in His heart.

Yeshua said, *"Is there anyone here who, if his son asks him for a loaf of bread, will give him a stone? or if he asks for a fish, will give him a snake?"* (Matthew 7:9-10). When we are walking in fellowship with our heavenly Father, the believer can have the utter confidence that God will hear and answer. This assurance is based on the character of God, our Father. On a human level, we know that if a son asks for bread, his father will not give him a stone. Neither would he give him a snake if he had asked for a fish. An earthly father would neither deceive his hungry son nor give him anything that might hurt him.

Yeshua then goes on to say in Matthew 7:11, *"So if you, even though you are bad, know how to give your children gifts that are good, how much more will your Father in heaven keep giving good things to those who keep asking him!"* Yeshua argues from the lesser to the greater. If human parents reward their children's requests with what is best for them, how much more will our Father who is in heaven do so.

I have met many sacrificially devoted parents. I have watched them pour out their lives for their children. It is quite beautiful, as well as commendable. God's love, on the other hand, is greater still. This supernatural divine love brought Yeshua to the execution stake. Now we are no longer enemies of God, but sons. How much more does God love His own.

Isaiah 53:10 says, *Yet it pleased ADONAI to crush him with illness, to see if he would present himself as a guilt offering. If he does, he will see his offspring.* The Lord saw fit to crush His one and only unique Son and put Him through agony. When His soul has been made an offering for sin, He will see His posterity, that is, all those who believe on Him. Seeing the multitudes of those who have been redeemed by His blood, He will be richly satisfied. This otherworldly, supernatural, divine, over-the-top love is hard to wrap our minds around, let alone receive. However, we must accept it and take it at face value if we are going to love the things that God loves.

Yeshua goes on to say in Matthew 7:12, *"Always treat others as you would like them to treat you; that sums up the teaching of the Torah and the Prophets."* The immediate connection of verse 12 with the preceding verse seems to be this: since our Father is a giver of good things to us, we should imitate Him in showing kindness to others. The way to test whether an action is beneficial to others is whether we would want to receive it ourselves. The Golden Rule

> *The way to test whether an action is beneficial to others is whether we would want to receive it ourselves.*

had been expressed in negative terms at least one hundred years before the time of Yeshua by Rabbi Hillel, who said, "Do not do to others what you would not have them do to you." However, by stating the rule in positive terminology, Yeshua goes beyond passive restraint to active benevolence. Our faith in Messiah Yeshua is not simply a matter of abstinence from sin; it is positive goodness.

John 13:33 says, *"Little children, I will be with you only a little longer. You will look for me; and, as I said to the Judeans, 'Where I am going, you cannot come,' now I say it to you as well."*

For the first time the Lord Yeshua addressed His disciples as *little children* – a term of endearment. And He used it only after Judas had departed. He was only to be with them a little while longer. Then He would die on the cross. They would seek Him then, but would not be able to follow Him, for He would return to heaven. The Lord had told the same thing to the Judeans, but He meant it in a different sense. For His disciples, His departure would only be temporary. He would come again for them (John chapter 14). But for those who didn't come to faith, His leaving them would be final. He was returning to heaven, and they could not follow Him because of their unbelief.

Yeshua goes on to say, *"I am giving you a new command: that you keep on loving each other. In the same way that I have loved you, you are also to keep on loving each other"* (John 13:34). During His absence, they were to be governed by the commandment of love. This commandment was not new at this time, because the Ten Commandments taught love to God and to one's neighbor. But this commandment was new in other ways, because the Holy Spirit would empower believers to obey it. It was new in that it was superior to the old. The old said, *Love your neighbor,* but the new said, *Love your enemies.*

It has been said that the law of love to others is now explained with new clarity, enforced by new motives and obligations, illustrated by a new example, and obeyed in a new way. Also, it was new, as explained in the verse, because it called for a higher degree of love: *"In the same way that I have loved you, you are also to keep on loving each other."* Can you imagine if we loved our brethren the way Yeshua loves us?

John 13:35 is the capstone of this section of Scripture, and says, *"Everyone will know that you are my talmidim* [disciples] *by the fact that you have love for each other."* The badge of the believer is not a cross worn around the neck, or on the lapel, or some distinctive type of clothing. Anyone could profess discipleship by these means. The true mark of a believer is love for his fellow believers. This requires divine power, and this power is only given to those indwelt by the Spirit.

First Peter 4:8 says, *More than anything, keep loving each other actively; because love covers many sins.* We must pay attention to our fellowship with other believers and have fervent love for all members of the household of faith. Such a love will not publicize the faults and failings of other believers but will protect them from public view. Someone has said, "Hatred makes the worst of everything. Love is entitled to bury things out of sight."

Romans 12:9-13 says, *Don't let love be a mere outward show. Recoil from what is evil, and cling to what is good. Love each other devotedly and with brotherly love; and set examples for each other in showing respect. Don't be lazy when hard work is needed, but serve the Lord with spiritual fervor. Rejoice in your hope, be patient in your troubles, and continue steadfastly in prayer. Share what you have with God's people, and practice hospitality.*

Verse 9 says, *Don't let love be a mere outward show. Recoil from what is evil, and cling to what is good.* Our love should be genuine and sincere, and we should hate all forms of evil and love what is good. In this setting, *evil* probably means all attitudes and acts of ill will, malice, and hatred. *Good,* by contrast, consists of every manifestation of supernatural love. The main tenant of Buddhism is to cease to do evil and do only good. The Bible said this about five hundred years before the advent of Buddhism, as it states in Psalm 34:14: *Turn from evil, and do good; seek peace, go after it!* Maybe the Buddha was perusing the Bible at some point in his life; I don't know. But what I do know is that it is the heart of God for His creation to cease from doing evil and live a life of goodness. The problem is that to accomplish this great feat, we will absolutely need power from on high. I personally studied many Eastern religions in the 1980s, and the things they were asking of me, although good in and of themselves, were not possible for me to accomplish in my own strength, or in anyone else's strength, for that matter. I tend to be an incredibly disciplined person, and I tried my absolute best. Little did I know, I desperately needed a savior.

Verse 10 says, *Love each other devotedly and with brotherly love; and set examples for each other in showing respect.* In our relations with those who are in the household of faith, we should demonstrate our love by tender affection, not by cool indifference or routine acceptance. We should prefer to see others honored rather than ourselves. Once a well-loved servant of Messiah Yeshua was in a side room with other notables before a meeting. Several had already moved onto the platform before it was his turn. When he appeared at the door, thunderous applause broke out for him. He quickly stepped aside and applauded so that he would not share the honor that he sincerely thought was intended for others.

We should demonstrate our love to those who are in the household of faith by tender affection, not by routine acceptance.

Verse 11 says, *Don't be lazy when hard work is needed, but serve the Lord with spiritual fervor.* In regard to this verse, James Moffat said, "Never let your zeal flag, maintain the spiritual glow, serve the Lord."[10] Here we are reminded of the words of Jeremiah 48:10: *A curse on him who does the work of ADONAI carelessly!*

Verse 12 says, *Rejoice in your hope, be patient in your troubles, and continue steadfastly in prayer.* No matter what our present circumstances may be, we can and should rejoice in hope, the coming of our Savior, the redemption of our bodies, and our eternal glory. We are exhorted to be patient in troubles, that is, to bear up bravely under them. Such all-conquering endurance is the one thing that can turn such misery into glory. We should continue steadfastly in prayer. It is in prayer that the work is done and victories are won. Prayer brings power in our lives and peace to our hearts. When we pray in the name of Yeshua, we come the closest to omnipotence that it is possible for mortal man to come. Therefore, we do ourselves a great disservice when we fail to pray.

Verse 13 says, *Share what you have with God's people, and practice hospitality.* Needy saints are everywhere – the unemployed, those who have been drained by medical bills, forgotten preachers and missionaries living in obscure places, and senior citizens whose resources have dwindled. True discipleship means sharing with those who are in need. Hospitality is a lost art. Small homes and apartments are used as excuses for not receiving believers who are passing through. Perhaps we do not want to face the added work and inconvenience. But we forget that when we entertain God's children, it is the same as if we were entertaining the Lord Himself. Our homes should be like the home in Bethany, where Yeshua loved to be.

---

10   James Moffat, *"New Testament, Romans,"* Online Bible, Bibliatodo, www.bibliatodo.com/en/the-bible/james-moffatt-new-testament/romans-12 (August 2022).

First John 4:20 says, *If anyone says, "I love God," and hates his brother, he is a liar. For if a person does not love his brother, whom he has seen, then he cannot love God, whom he has not seen.* John emphasizes the futility of professing to love God while at the same time hating one's brother. As spokes of a wheel get nearer to the center, so they get nearer to one another. Thus, as we get closer to the Lord, the more we will love our fellow believers.

Actually, we do not love the Lord a bit more than we love the humblest of His followers. John argues the impossibility of loving God whom we have not seen if we do not love our brothers whom we have seen. I tend to go out of my way for the lost. I have this burning desire in my heart to see none perish, but for all to come to everlasting life. I'm not sure I do the same for the body of Messiah. I tend to have high expectations for the body. There is a danger in having too high of expectations, for when reality sets in, you usually end up with disappointment. We have to learn to be just as loving to the lost as we are to the body of Yeshua. We should never ask God to look at us through the eyes of mercy, and then look at our brothers and sisters through the eyes of the law. If we're going to love what God loves, then we need to love all believers too.

CHAPTER 13

GOD LOVES THOSE WHO
DO WHAT IS RIGHT

*A*DONAI *detests the way of the wicked but loves anyone who pursues righteousness.* (Proverbs 15:9 CJB)

The L*ORD *detests the way of the wicked, but he loves those who pursue godliness.* (Proverbs 15:9 NLT)

The way of the wicked is an abomination to the L*ORD, *but He loves the one who pursues righteousness.* (Proverbs 15:9 NASB)

Any way you slice it or dice it, the way of the wicked displeases the Lord greatly. He loves the person who lives in obedience to His Word. The Lord is perfectly holy. Isaiah 6:3-4 says, *They were crying out to each other, "More holy than the holiest holiness is* A*DONAI-Tzva'ot *[The Lord of Heaven's Armies]!*

The whole earth is filled with his glory!" The doorposts shook at the sound of their shouting, and the house was filled with smoke.

They are seraphim, majestic celestial beings with six wings – four wings for reverence and two wings for service in attendance upon God. They were calling to one another, describing God as *more holy than the holiest holiness.* There is none as holy as the Lord our God. His holiness is beyond explanation. It is a perfect holiness, which defies any intelligible language the ability to describe Him. In fact, when the prophet Isaiah saw a vision of the Lord sitting high on a lofty throne, it produced a deep conviction of sin in him, which then brought him to the place of confession. Leviticus 20:7 says, *"Therefore consecrate yourselves – you people must be holy, because I am ADONAI your God."* Because God is holy, it is necessary for His people to be holy as well.

> *Yeshua pronounces a blessing on those who hunger and thirst for righteousness.*

Matthew 5:6 states, *"How blessed are those who hunger and thirst for righteousness! for they will be filled."* Yeshua pronounces a blessing on those who hunger and thirst for righteousness: They are promised satisfaction. These people have a passion for righteousness in their own lives; they long to see honesty, integrity, and justice in society; they look for practical holiness in the body of Messiah, the church. Like the people of whom Gamaliel Bradford wrote, they have "a thirst no earthly stream can satisfy, a hunger that must feed on Messiah or die." These people will be abundantly satisfied in Messiah's coming kingdom; they shall be filled, for righteousness will reign and corruption will give way to the highest moral standards. Surely leading a righteous life has its own reward, but what greater reward is there than to be the object of God's love.

First Peter 1:14-16 says, *As people who obey God, do not let yourselves be shaped by the evil desires you used to have when you were still ignorant. On the contrary, following the Holy One who called you, become holy yourselves in your entire way of life; since the Tanakh* [Old Testament] *says, "You are to be holy because I am holy."*

The subject here is obedience. Obedient children should not indulge in the sins that characterized them in their former life. Now that they are believers, they should pattern their lives after the One whose name they bear. If they conform to the ungodly world, they are denying their heavenly character. The things they did in the days of their ignorance should be put away now that they have been illuminated by the Holy Spirit. The former lusts are the sins they indulged in while they were still ignorant of God. To indulge in them now would be a willful ignorance and would not be considered a born-again lifestyle.

Instead of imitating the ungodly world with its fads and fashions, our lives should reproduce the holy character of the One who called us. To be godly means to be God-like. God is holy in all His ways. If we are to be like Him, we must be holy in all that we do and say. In this life we will never be as holy as He is, but we should be holy because He is holy. Peter reaches back into the Old Testament for proof that God expects His people to be like Himself.

In Leviticus 11:44, the Lord said, *"For I am Adonai your God; therefore, consecrate yourselves and be holy, for I am holy; and do not defile yourselves with any kind of swarming creature that moves along the ground."* Believers are empowered to live holy lives by the indwelling Holy Spirit. Old Testament saints did not have this help and blessing, but since we are more privileged, we are also more responsible. *"From him who has been given much, much will be demanded — from someone to whom people entrust much, they ask still more"* (Luke 12:48). Those who have come to know God's will as it is revealed in the Scriptures are under great responsibility to obey it. Much has been given to them; much will be required of them.

The verse Peter quotes from Leviticus acquires a new depth of meaning in the New Testament. It is the difference between the formal and the vital. Holiness was God's ideal in the Old Testament, but it has assumed a concrete, everyday quality with the coming of the Spirit of truth. The word *righteousness* or *righteous* occurs about five hundred times in the Bible. *Righteousness* can be defined broadly as "morally acceptable behavior." Biblically, those who are righteous are acceptable to God, as made possible by God. *Righteousness* conveys a sense of justice, justness, or divine holiness. God is the standard of righteousness.

To be righteous is to be right with God. So another name for *righteousness* is *rightness.* The righteousness of Messiah is imputed or ascribed to us when we are saved, yet it is also something we are called to pursue. We are called to live for righteousness. There is a vast difference between positional righteousness and practical righteousness. At the moment of salvation, we are sanctified or set apart *positionally;* that is, we are saved from the ultimate penalty of sin. This is known as positional righteousness, when we are set free from sin's penalty.

Then begins progressive sanctification, or progressive righteousness, the process whereby we are saved from the practice and power of sin. This is known as practical righteousness or being set free from the power of sin in our everyday lives. We need to make our condition more like our position. This is a magnificent process accomplished by submitting our will to the power of the Holy Spirit, whereby the supernatural becomes more natural, and the natural becomes more unnatural.

Sometimes we miss the forest for the trees, especially when we get lost in ecumenical theological terminology. Simply stated, God loves those who practice righteousness, which is spiritual rightness. Why is God so adamant about His children following His ways? For the same reason we as parents are so adamant about our children following our ways – because we love them and only want the best for them. We want them to be protected; we want them to prosper; and we want them to know and have peace. This is exactly what God wants for His children as well. The walls and boundaries set in place for us are not set up to keep us from leaving; rather, they are set in place to prevent the enemy from coming in and destroying our lives.

The boundaries set in place for us are not to keep us from leaving; rather, they are to prevent the enemy from coming in.

God loves the righteous, but He detests the way of the wicked. The person who leads a life of persistent sin is guilty of doing what the Lord hates. His actions are distasteful to the Lord; the Hebrew term is often translated as *abomination.* Romans 1:18

warns that *what is revealed is God's anger from heaven against all the godlessness and wickedness of people who in their wickedness keep suppressing the truth.* Here we have the answer to the question, Why do men need the gospel? The answer is that they are lost without it, and that the wrath of God is revealed from heaven against the wickedness of men who suppress the truth in an unrighteous manner and by their unrighteous lives.

But how is God's wrath revealed? One answer is given in the context of Romans 1. God gives men over to uncleanness (verse 24), to shameful desires (verse 26), and to foolish thinking (verse 28). But it is also true that God breaks through into history to show His displeasure at man's sin: for example, the flood (Genesis 7), the destruction of Sodom and Gomorrah (Genesis 19), and the punishment of Korah, Dathan, and Abiram (Numbers 16). Sadly, this is also a precursor to the ultimate judgment at the end of time for those who don't turn from their unrighteousness. This is why God wants all men to be free, redeemed, and walking on the road of righteousness, for the Lord is good and wants none to perish, but for all to come to everlasting life.

God's laws are ways of protection, prosperity, and peace. The law of God is the wisdom from God. Proverbs 3:1 says, *My son, don't forget my teaching, keep my commands in your heart.* Like all good parents, wisdom wants the best for her children. She knows that it can come only through obedience to her teachings, which is another way of saying obedience to the sacred Scriptures, so she pleads with her son to remember with the mind and obey with the heart. This is another way of doing what is right. If we are going to love what God loves, then we need to love right and do right, even if no one else does.

CHAPTER 14

GOD LOVES THOSE WHO
OBEY HIS WORD

Deuteronomy 7:9 says, *"From this you can know that Adonai your God is indeed God, the faithful God, who keeps his covenant and extends grace to those who love him and observe his mitzvot* [commandments], *to a thousand generations."*

God had chosen Israel to be a people who were separated unto Himself. He did not want them to be like the other nations. He did not choose them because of their superior numbers. *"Adonai didn't set his heart on you or choose you because you numbered more than any other people – on the contrary, you were the fewest of all peoples"* (Deuteronomy 7:7).

He chose them simply because He loved them, and He wanted them to obey Him in all things. *"Rather, it was because Adonai loved you, and because he wanted to keep the oath which he had sworn to your ancestors, that* Adonai *brought you out with a strong hand and redeemed you from a life of slavery under the hand of Pharaoh king of Egypt"* (Deuteronomy 7:8).

The meaning of *a thousand generations* is forever. This is a constant theme in the Bible:

> *I prayed to* Adonai *my God and made this confession: "Please, Adonai, great and fearsome God, who keeps his covenant and extends grace to those who love him and observe his mitzvot!"* (Daniel 9:4)

> *I said, "Please,* Adonai! *God of heaven! You great and fearsome God, who keeps his covenant and extends grace to those who love him and observe his mitzvot!"* (Nehemiah 1:5)

> *"You are to have no other gods before me. You are not to make for yourselves a carved image or any kind of representation of anything in heaven above, on the earth beneath or in the water below the shoreline. You are not to bow down to them or serve them; for I,* Adonai *your God, am a jealous God, punishing the children for the sins of the parents to the third and fourth generation of those who hate me, but displaying grace to the thousandth generation of those who love me and obey my mitzvot."* (Exodus 20:3-6)

> Psalm 103:17-18 says, *But the mercy of* Adonai *on those who fear him is from eternity past to eternity future, and his righteousness extends to his*

*children's children, provided they keep his covenant
and remember to follow his precepts.*

With God's mercy there is a vivid contrast. It lasts from everlasting to everlasting to those who fear Him. In duration, as
in volume, it is limitless. And His righteousness extends to
his children's children. There is a great comfort in this, for
believing parents often feel concern about their children and
grandchildren growing up in a world
of mounting wickedness. But we can *God's promises are valid*
safely entrust our little ones to the *for those who keep His*
One whose love is infinite and whose *covenant and remember*
righteousness is sufficient not only for *His commandments*
us but for succeeding generations as *to do them.*
well. Of course, the promises neces-
sarily have a condition attached. They are valid for those who
keep His covenant and remember His commandments to do
them. But that is only reasonable.

Our God and the God of our fathers is a blesser. The very
first act He performed after creating man was that He blessed
them: *So God created humankind in his own image; in the
image of God he created him: male and female he created them.
God blessed them: God said to them, "Be fruitful, multiply, fill
the earth and subdue it. Rule over the fish in the sea, the birds
in the air and every living creature that crawls on the earth"*
(Genesis 1:27-28).

The very last words out of Yeshua's mouth prior to His
ascension back to heaven were a blessing over His disciples:
He led them out toward Beit-Anyah; then, raising his hands,

he said a b'rakhah [blessing] *over them; and as he was blessing them, he withdrew from them and was carried up into heaven* (Luke 24:50-51).

The Bible ends with a blessing, as stated in the very last verse: *May the grace of the Lord Yeshua be with all!* (Revelation 22:21).

The point here is that God is good, and His mercy endures forever. His desire is for His children to be blessed. To think that rewards are not attached to responsibility would be foolhardy, but this is a social epidemic we are currently suffering from. God made it abundantly clear in Leviticus chapter 26 and Deuteronomy chapter 28 that there are blessings attached to obedience to God's commands, and sadly but rightfully so, there are curses attached to disobedience to God's commands. This is the only way for any society to operate practically. There is no logical, reasonable, stable human being who can deny that if more and more people chose to obey the ways of God, the world in which we live wouldn't be a more beautiful and glorious place to live. I'm reminded of what my late great bubbe (grandmother) would always say to me: "My child, the world is a beautiful place, it's the people that make it ugly."

As the people of God, we have the distinct opportunity as well as a spiritual responsibility to not only tell the world about our great and awesome God, but also to tell of His ways and the need to obey them. If we are going to represent God and be His ambassadors on this earth, then we have to emulate Him in word, thought, deed, and action. He deserves the very best of us in terms of representation.

In the midst of prayer one day, I was overwhelmed with the Lord's goodness, love, grace, and mercy in the willingness to give

His only begotten Son to an underserving sinful world. I said to the Lord, "I don't understand something. You are so good, and so incredibly gracious; why don't more people believe in you and love you?" To which He answered, "Bad representation."

This concept is not just an Old Testament religious philosophy; it is the way of life for the believer. Yeshua said, *"If you love me, you will keep my commands"* (John 14:15; cf. 14:21, 23). The Lord Yeshua was about to leave His disciples, and they would be filled with sorrow. How would they be able to express their love to Him? The answer was by keeping His commandments. Not by tears, but by obedience.

I think some of us may be under the impression that the Father's commands and Yeshua's commands are different. But I beg to differ. If the Father's commands and Yeshua's commands differ, then how could Yeshua claim to be one with the Father? (John 10:30). In a two-parent household, it is imperative that both parents are on the same page when it comes to rules and regulations as they apply to their children, for a house divided will fall.

Romans 7:12 says, *So the Torah is holy; that is, the commandment is holy, just and good.* Here the apostle Paul tells us that the law itself is holy, and each commandment is holy and just and good. We must constantly remember that there is nothing wrong with the law, for it was given by God and therefore is perfect as an expression of His will for His people. The weakness of the law lay in the "raw materials" it had to work with; it was given to people who were already sinners. They needed the law to give them the knowledge of sin, for sin is lawlessness (1 John 3:4). Sin or lawlessness is insubordination to God, wanting one's own way and refusing to acknowledge the Lord as rightful sovereign. In essence, it is placing one's own will above the will of God. It is opposition to a living person who has the right to be obeyed.

Romans 7:13 says, *Then did something good become for me the source of death? Heaven forbid! Rather, it was sin working death in me through something good, so that sin might be clearly exposed as sin, so that sin through the commandment might come to be experienced as sinful beyond measure.*

What is good refers to the law, as is specifically stated in the preceding verse. Paul raises the question, Did the law become death to me? which means, is the law the culprit, dooming Paul and all the rest of us to death? The answer, of course, is certainly not! Sin is the culprit. The law didn't originate sin, but it showed sin in all its exceeding sinfulness. By the law is the knowledge of sin (Romans 3:20). But that is not all! How does man's sinful nature respond when God's holy law forbids it to do something? The answer is familiar. What may have been dormant desire now becomes a burning passion! This sin becomes exceedingly sinful through the commandment.

The law can reveal sin, just as a thermometer reveals the temperature. But it cannot control sin like a thermostat controls the temperature.

There might seem to be a contradiction between what Paul says here and in Romans 7:10 where he said he found the law to bring death. Here he denies that the law became death to him. The solution is this: The law by itself can neither improve the old nature on the one hand, nor cause it to sin on the other. It can reveal sin, just as a thermometer reveals the temperature. But it cannot control sin like a thermostat controls the temperature.

A mirror can show a person what needs to be cleaned up, but it cannot do the cleaning.

But what happens is this: Man's fallen human nature instinctively wants to do whatever is forbidden. It uses the law to awaken otherwise dormant lusts in the sinner's life. The more man tries, the worse it gets, until at last he is brought to despair of all hope. Thus, sin uses the law to cause any hope of improvement to die in him. And he sees the exceeding sinfulness of his old nature as he never saw it before.

The subject of holy living – obeying God's commands – continues in Romans chapter 8. In chapter 6, Paul had answered the question, Does the teaching of the gospel (salvation by faith alone) permit or even encourage sinful living? In chapter 7, he faced up to the question, Does the gospel tell believers to keep the law in order to live a holy life? Now the question in chapter 8 is, How is the believer enabled to live a holy life?

Being born again and filled with the Holy Spirit is the only way. Just as it was instinctive to live an unholy life prior to the new birth, it should be just as instinctive to live a holy life once the new birth has taken place.

Obedience to God is something we do which demonstrates our love towards Him. The greatest love is love by decision, not by feelings. Obedience is the key to God's heart, but love turns the key. That's why Deuteronomy 6:5 says, *"You are to love ADONAI your God with all your heart, all your being and all your resources."* And to love God is to obey God lovingly.

Proverbs 3:5-6 says, *Trust in ADONAI with all your heart; do not rely on your own understanding. In all your ways acknowledge him; then he will level your paths.* First, there must be a full commitment of ourselves – spirit, soul, and body – to the Lord. We must trust Him not only for the salvation of our souls but also for the direction of our lives. It must be a commitment without reserve. Next, there must be a healthy distrust of self, an acknowledgement that we do not know what is best for us, that we are not capable of guiding ourselves. Jeremiah said it well: *ADONAI, I know that the way of humans is not in their control, humans are not able to direct their steps as they walk* (Jeremiah 10:23).

Finally, there must be an acknowledgement of the lordship of Yeshua: *In all your ways acknowledge him.* Every area of our lives must be turned over to His control. We must have no will of our own, only a single, pure desire to know His will and to do it. If we meet these conditions, God promises that He will direct our paths. There are many ways He can accomplish this. He may do it through the Bible, through the advice of mature, God-fearing believers, through the amazing convergence of circumstances, through the inward peace of the Spirit, or through a combination of these things. But if we wait, He will make the guidance so clear that to refuse would be positive disobedience.

If we wait, God will make the guidance so clear that to refuse would be positive disobedience.

When I first met the Lord, I was well aware that He was God and I was not. I knew that He knew all things, and in actuality, I knew little to nothing. That encounter caused me to feel infinitesimal. I actually made a pact with God. Little did I know that God was a covenant-making and a covenant-keeping God. I said, "If You make things clear to me, I will do it." By the same token, we have the Word of God, which plainly spells out what God loves and what God hates. If we obey God's ways, we will love what He loves and hate what He hates.

Psalm 119:100 says, *I understand more than my elders, because I keep your precepts.* This may sound like irresponsible boasting, but it is not so. It is not a person's age or intelligence that matters, but his obedience. The youth may outstrip the aged if he has a higher OQ (Obedience Quotient). If we are going to love what God loves, we need to respect His Word, His ways, and His Spirit, and obey Him always!

CHAPTER 15

GOD LOVES THOSE WHO TREAT OTHERS FAIRLY

P salm 37:28 says, *For Adonai loves justice and will not abandon his faithful; they are preserved forever. But the descendants of the wicked will be cut off.*

The Lord loves justice, and it is in keeping with His justice that He makes His children eternally secure. It is not that we deserve eternal life, but that Messiah died to purchase it for us and that God must honor the terms of the purchase. Why does He have to honor the terms of the purchase? Because not only does God love justice, but He Himself also is in fact just.

Deuteronomy 32:4 says, *The Rock! His work is perfect, for all his ways are just. A trustworthy God who does no wrong, he is righteous and straight.* The justice of God can be defined as "that essential and infinite attribute which makes his nature and his ways the perfect embodiment of equity, and constitutes him the model and the guardian of equity throughout the universe" (*American Tract Society Bible Dictionary*, 1859). The word for *just* in the Hebrew is *tzaddik*. In strict orthodox Judaism, calling one a *tzaddik* is a high complement. It means the person is just, lawful, and righteous. When referring to God, it means He is perfect, correct, and right in *all* His ways, and in *all* He does. In fact, Messiah Yeshua is the ultimate *Tzaddik*.

Psalm 11:7 says, *For ADONAI is righteous; he loves righteousness; the upright will see his face.* Just as God hates the violent man, so he loves the righteous. God Himself is righteous, and He loves righteousness. The ultimate reward of the upright will be to stand in God's presence. *Better a day in your courtyards than a thousand [days elsewhere]. Better just standing at the door of my God's house than living in the tents of the wicked* (Psalm 84:11).

In order to understand God's justice, we must first understand sin. First John 3:4 says, *Everyone who keeps sinning is violating Torah [Law] – indeed, sin is violation of Torah*. In other words, sin is lawlessness. Sin embodies everything that is contrary to God's holy nature. Thus, sin is a crime not only against the law, but also against the Lord Himself, and it demands the death penalty. But God in His infinite mercy and amazing grace sent His Son, the Lord Yeshua, to pay the penalty.

In God's economy, the penalty for sin cannot be overlooked; it's either judged or forgiven.

In God's economy, the penalty for sin cannot be overlooked; it's either judged or forgiven. Atonement, or *kawfar* in the Hebrew, only happens when the sin is paid for. But who can legitimately pay for all that sin? Not a human being. So God provides an innocent victim to be slaughtered as a substitute, known as a *zawbak,* so His righteous judgment can be transferred and satisfied. Justice satisfied, love uncompromised. In other words, God's love provided what His holiness demanded. It should blow us away that we have a *Tzaddik,* Yeshua, as our righteous defender.

First John 2:1 says, *My children, I am writing you these things so that you won't sin. But if anyone does sin, we have Yeshua the Messiah, the Tzaddik, who pleads our cause with the Father.* John gives us God's perfect standard for His people and His gracious provision in the event of failure. Because God is perfect, His standard for His people is perfection. He would not be God if He said, "I am writing these things so that you sin as little as you can." God cannot condone sin in the least degree, so He sets perfection before us as the goal.

Yeshua did this with the woman caught in adultery. He said to her, *"Neither do I condemn you. Now go, and don't sin any more"* (John 8:11). At the same time, God knows our frame. He remembers that we are dust, so He has graciously made provision for us in the event of failure. This is expressed in the words, *If anyone does sin, we have Yeshua the Messiah, the Tzaddik, who pleads our cause with the Father.* This is exactly what the Lord Yeshua does for us when we sin. He immediately comes to us in order to restore us to fellowship with Himself. Notice that this verse doesn't say, *If anyone confesses his sins.* As our advocate, Yeshua seeks to bring us to the place where we do confess and forsake our sin. Yeshua doesn't wait for us to come to him. He initiates the broken fellowship by alerting us through the Spirit.

Notice that our advocate is Messiah Yeshua the *Tzaddik* (the Righteous). When satan brings some accusation against us, Messiah Yeshua can point to His finished work on Golgotha and say, "Charge that to My account," thereby giving us what we don't deserve and at the same time withholding from us that which we do deserve. This is the fullness of mercy and grace. *The Word became a human being and lived with us, and we saw his Sh'khinah* [Glory], *the Sh'khinah of the Father's only Son, full of grace and truth* (John 1:14).

It is because God is just that we desperately need to follow in His footsteps and live justly as well. Having been made in His image (Genesis 1:26-27), we human beings long for moral justice to prevail upon the earth, and we are outraged when we see injustice happening all around us. Why do we seek justice for crimes? It is in our spiritual DNA to seek justice, because we are made in the image of a just God.

Justice is a major theme in Scripture, which contains many calls for justice, and commands to worship God for His justice. It has to do with conduct in relation to others. Just behavior accords with what is morally right and fair. Justice is the quality of doing what is right.

Scripture is full of commands that humans act justly. This includes acting on behalf of those whose rights are being denied and those who are powerless to defend themselves. Isaiah 1:17 says, *"Learn to do good! Seek justice, relieve the oppressed, defend orphans, plead for the widow."* The prophet Isaiah tells the people of Israel that they need to wash themselves from sin through the cleansing waters of repentance and forsaking of evil; then they should practice righteousness and social justice.

We, as the believing community, cannot just teach on the subject. Our character has to line up with our creed. We have to be intentional about taking care of the poor, the widow, and the orphan. As a parent of children you are raising in the faith, don't just teach your children the Scripture, but also show your children the Scripture by obeying the command and thereby acting justly. What do you think would have more of an impact – teaching your children to memorize the verse that says, *The religious observance that God the Father considers pure and faultless is this: to care for orphans and widows in their distress and to keep oneself from being contaminated by the world* (James 1:27), or to take your children and physically care for orphans and widows in their pain and sorrow?

> *Don't just teach your children the Scripture, but also show your children the Scripture by obeying the command.*

Isaiah 10:1-2 says, *Woe to those who enact unjust decrees and draft oppressive legislation to deprive the impoverished of justice and rob my people's poor of their rights, looting widows and preying on orphans!* A threatening, lamenting, and admonishing woe is pronounced on those rulers who rob the needy, oppress the poor, and write unjust decrees. When the judgment of God falls, they will lose all the wealth they gained through illegal means and extortion.

Jeremiah 22:3 says, *This is what ADONAI says: "Do what is right and just; rescue the wronged from their oppressors; do nothing wrong or violent to the stranger, orphan or widow; don't shed innocent blood in this place."* Here the prophet warns King Zedekiah of Judah to dispense justice and righteousness;

otherwise, Judah, though as magnificent as Gilead and Lebanon, will be stripped bare and depopulated.

Psalm 82:2-4 says, *"How long will you go on judging unfairly, favoring the wicked? Give justice to the weak and fatherless! Uphold the rights of the wretched and poor! Rescue the destitute and needy; deliver them from the power of the wicked!"* In this psalm, earth's rulers are on trial. The judge has taken His seat at the bench. God Himself has called a special session of the divine council in order to reprove the rulers and judges of the earth. First God rebukes them for their violation of their public trust in office. They have been guilty of the acquisition of gain or advantage by dishonest, unfair, or illegal means, especially through the abuse of their position or influence in politics. They are guilty of corruption. Under their administration, the rich have been favored while the poor have been oppressed. Criminals have escaped unpunished, and the innocent have had to suffer loss without recourse. The scales of justice have become the scales of oppression.

Then the judge of all the earth reminds them once more of their responsibilities in the area of social justice. They are to champion the rights of the poor and the fatherless, the afflicted and the needy. They should be helpers of all who are dispossessed and downtrodden. This was written three thousand years ago, but it is just as applicable to the time we currently live in. As Solomon said, *There is nothing new under the sun* (Ecclesiastes 1:9).

The Torah (Mosaic law) specifically speaks out for justice. Leviticus 19:35-36 says, *"Don't be dishonest when measuring length, weight or capacity. Rather, use an honest balance-scale, honest weights, an honest bushel dry-measure and an honest gallon liquid-measure; I am* ADONAI *your God, who brought you out of the land of Egypt."*

God is calling on all believers to practice honesty in business.

Exodus 23:8 says, *You are not to receive a bribe, for a bribe blinds the clearsighted and subverts the cause of the righteous.* God is commanding His people to show no partiality by receiving a bribe.

God places a special responsibility on judges and other authorities to provide justice, warning them in Psalm 82 that they will themselves face judgment. Every human tribunal is under God's order to do what is right:

> *"Do not be unjust in judging – show neither partiality to the poor nor deference to the mighty, but with justice judge your neighbor."* (Leviticus 19:15)

> *"In the past* ADONAI*-Tzva'ot said, 'Administer true justice. Let everyone show mercy and compassion to his brother.'"* (Zechariah 7:9)

> *"You are not to show favoritism when judging, but give equal attention to the small and to the great. No matter how a person presents himself, don't be afraid of him; because the decision is God's. The case that is too hard for you, bring to me and I will hear it."* (Deuteronomy 1:17)

> *"Do not deny anyone justice in his lawsuit simply because he is poor."* (Exodus 23:6)

*"Justice, only justice, you must pursue; so that you
will live and inherit the land* ADONAI *your God is
giving you."* (Deuteronomy 16:20)

We all have a sense of right and wrong; however, our individual
sense of right and wrong can be skewed. For instance, when
I first moved to Florida, I decided to get involved with prison
ministry. I read in the Bible: *Remember those in prison and being
mistreated, as if you were in prison with them and undergoing
their torture yourselves* (Hebrews 13:3). I also thought about
how sad it must be to be incarcerated. I'll never forget my first
visit. My shoulders rose and I turned around every time I felt
a cell door close behind me. It was eerie, to say the least. I felt
as though *I* was in prison, and it was an ugly feeling and made
me very uncomfortable.

I had not received any training nor instruction on what is
appropriate or inappropriate when talking with the inmates.
I asked the first man what he was in for. He said he had killed
his wife. I asked him how he felt about it, and the man showed
absolutely no remorse. I was shocked. I asked him how he felt
about someone who commits pedophilia. At this point in the
conversation, he got enraged and said immediately in a crazy,
harsh tone that he would kill that person. This is when I realized that everyone, unless they are mentally incompetent or
unstable, has some sense of right and wrong. Although this right
and wrong tends to be subjective, especially today in a society
where most people claim that there is no absolute truth, known
as the principle of relativism, we as the body of Messiah known
better. As believers, we must get our sense of right and wrong

from God's laws, for this is truth. *"Set them apart for holiness by means of the truth — your word is truth"* (John 17:17). We must not only know the truth but act upon it as well. Justice and righteousness are not just a philosophy, but a way of life. The Bible tells us that we must act justly.

The righteous understands the cause of the poor, but the wicked is unconcerned (Proverbs 29:7). Believers, righteous people, take an active interest in the poor. Wicked people couldn't care less.

Justice and righteousness are not just a philosophy, but a way of life.

Evil people don't understand justice, but those who seek ADONAI *understand everything* (Proverbs 28:5). By refusing to practice justice, evil men prove that they don't understand justice, and they lose the power to understand it.

From under a cloak a bad man takes a bribe to pervert the course of justice (Proverbs 17:23). A wicked man accepts a bribe behind the back to influence the decision of a judge in his favor.

How happy are those who act justly, who always do what is right! (Psalm 106:3). It feels so right to do the right thing.

Romans 12:19 says, *Never seek revenge, my friends; instead, leave that to God's anger; for in the Tanakh* [Old Testament] *it is written, "*ADONAI *says, 'Vengeance is my responsibility; I will repay.'"* We must resist the tendency to avenge wrongs that are done to us. The expression, *Leave that to God's anger,* means to allow God to take care of it for you. Vengeance is God's prerogative. We should not interfere with what is His right. He will repay at the proper time and in the proper manner. Lenski writes, "God has long ago settled the whole matter about exacting justice from wrongdoers. Not one of them will escape. Perfect justice will be done in every case and will be done perfectly. If any of us interfered, it would be the height of presumption."

Ultimately, by acting justly and according to God's ways, God is protecting me from you and you from me. Since God is a blesser of men, we desperately need to follow in His footsteps by acting justly. Try not to focus on all that is wrong in our world and just do what's right and just. I remember when I first got married, someone asked me if I was going to have children, to which I emphatically responded with a resounding yes! They asked why I would want to bring children into this dark and broken world in which we live, to which I exclaimed, "In order to help change the spiritual climate of this dark and broken world in which we live." I explained to the man that my plan was to train my children in the ways of God, and through their just behavior they would bring light and restoration to this dark and broken world.

Psalm 11 says,

> In ADONAI I find refuge. So how can you say to
> me, "Flee like a bird to the mountains! See how the
> wicked are drawing their bows and setting their
> arrows on the string, to shoot from the shadows at
> honest men. If the foundations are destroyed, what
> can the righteous do?" ADONAI is in his holy temple.
> ADONAI, his throne is in heaven. His eyes see and
> test humankind. ADONAI tests the righteous; but he
> hates the wicked and the lover of violence. He will
> rain hot coals down on the wicked, fire, sulfur and
> scorching wind will be what they get to drink. For

*ADONAI is righteous; he loves righteousness; the
upright will see his face.*

There are many gloomy headlines these days. When the news
is all bad – wars, violence, crime, corruption, injustice, and
political unrest – David reminds us that we can rise above the
circumstances of life by keeping our eyes on the Lord. The Lord
has promised to return and set things
right. Truth will win in the end, so we
need not get all upset over the headlines.
The waves of adverse circumstances

*The Lord has promised
to return and set
things right.*

may seem to be against us at any particular time, but the tide
of God's irresistible purpose is sure to win in the end. In the
meantime, if we are going to love what God loves, we need to be
just and fair toward others and in every situation operate justly.

CHAPTER 16

GOD LOVES A CHEERFUL GIVER

Second Corinthians 9:7 says, *Each should give according to what he has decided in his heart, not grudgingly or under compulsion, for God loves a cheerful giver.*

Each one is to give as he purposes in his heart. It will be necessary for him to consider what is necessary for his own immediate needs. He will have to think only of obligations that he will incur in the course of normal life. But then, beyond that, he should think of the needs of his fellow believers and of the claims of Messiah upon him. Reviewing all these considerations, he should give not grudgingly or out of necessity. It is possible to give and yet not be happy about it. It is also possible to give under pressure of emotional appeals or public embarrassment. None of these things will do. God blesses a cheerful giver. It has often been pointed out that our word *hilarious* comes from the word translated *cheerful* from the Greek word *hilarion,* which means "cheerful."

Does God really need our money? No, the cattle on a thousand hills belong to Him, and if He needed anything, He would not tell us (Psalm 50:10-12). But our heart's attitude is what is important to Him. God had never intended right outward action to serve as a cover for wrong inward attitudes. God loves to see a believer who is so filled with the joy of the Lord that he wants to share what he has with others.

God loves a cheerful giver because, as Jowett says, "Cheerful giving is born of love, and therefore it is a lover loving a lover and rejoicing in the communion. Giving is the language of loving; indeed, it has no other speech. God so loved the world that He gave! Love finds its very life in giving itself away. Its only pride in possession is the joy of surrender. If love has all things, it yet possesses nothing."[11]

Isaiah 53:10 says, *It pleased ADONAI to crush him with illness, to see if he would present himself as a guilt offering. If he does, he will see his offspring.* God gave cheerfully and not begrudgingly. If we are going to become more like God, then we have to become more of a cheerful giver. We can learn to be more of a cheerful giver by emulating God. Not only did God give the greatest gift ever in Messiah Yeshua, but the gift itself gave as well.

Philippians 2:5-8 says, *Let your attitude toward one another be governed by your being in union with the Messiah Yeshua: Though he was in the form of God, he did not regard equality with God something to be possessed by force. On the contrary, he emptied himself, in that he took the form of a slave by becoming like human beings are. And when he appeared as a human*

---

11 John Henry Jowett, *Life in the Heights: Studies in the Epistles* (London: Hodder and Stoughton, 1924).

being, he humbled himself still more by becoming obedient even to death – death on a stake as a criminal!

Yeshua had the selfless mind, the sacrificial mind, and the serving mind. He constantly thought of others and gave cheerfully. Even as he approached a horrifically painful death on behalf of others, He said, *"Father, if you are willing, take this cup away from me; still, let not my will but yours be done"* (Luke 22:42).

Romans 8:29 says, *Those whom he knew in advance, he also determined in advance would be conformed to the pattern of his Son, so that he might be the firstborn among many brothers.* God has predestined His children to be conformed to the likeness of His Son; therefore, by giving selflessly we can become more like Yeshua. Our greatest motivation for cheerful and generous giving is simply to please the Lord and reflect His image in our lives. Our God is a giving God. He is a God of abundance (John 10:10; James 1:5; Psalm 103:8; Isaiah 55:1-7; 2 Corinthians 9:8; Romans 5:20), and He loves to give. He sacrificed willingly on the cross and then invited us into fullness of life. As His children, we are called to imitate Him (Ephesians 5:1). Our generosity in giving is a demonstration of God's character and a response to what He has done for us.

> *Our greatest motivation for cheerful giving is simply to please the Lord and reflect His image in our lives.*

Second Corinthians 9:6 says, *Here's the point: he who plants sparingly also harvests sparingly.* In 2 Corinthians 9:6-15, the apostle Paul lists some of the wonderful rewards and benefits of giving as a believer. First, he sets forth the law of the harvest. It's a well-known fact in agriculture that a generous sowing of seed is necessary if there is to be a generous harvest. Perhaps the farmer is ready to put the seed in the ground. Shall he sow liberally or shall he sow sparingly? The thought here is that if he sows liberally, he will also reap liberally, but if he sows sparingly, he will also reap sparingly.

We should also remember this with regard to agriculture – the farmer does not reap the exact amount of grain he sows, but much more, proportionately. So it is with the believer's giving; it is not a question of receiving back exactly what one has given, but receiving back far more out of proportion to the amount of the gift. Of course, the return is not as much in money as in spiritual blessings.

Acts 20:35 says, *"In everything I have given you an example of how, by working hard like this, you must help the weak, remembering the words of the Lord Yeshua himself, 'There is more happiness in giving than in receiving.'"* During Paul's third missionary journey, he closes his message with an element of his own life. He could say in all honesty that he did not covet anyone's silver or gold. He was not motivated by financial gain in his work for the Lord. Essentially, he was a poor man according to the world's standards, but so rich toward God. He reminded them that he worked as a tentmaker to provide for his own needs as well as the needs of those who were with him. The elders should remember this and in all things seek the good of others, remembering the words of Yeshua: *"It is more blessed to give than to receive"* (Acts 20:35 NKJV). Interestingly enough, these words of our Lord are not found in any of the Gospels. They do, however, represent the sum of much of His teaching, but here they are given as an inspired addition to His words in the Gospels.

Proverbs 22:9 says, *He who is generous is blessed, because he shares his food with the poor.* The generous man is blessed in showing benevolence to others. By sharing his substance with the poor, he gains present happiness and future reward. No one can deny that giving makes a person happy. For the believer, not only do we gain happiness in this present life, but we also attain rewards in the life to come, whereby in giving, we store up treasures in heaven.

Matthew 6:19-21 says, *"Do not store up for yourselves wealth here on earth, where moths and rust destroy, and burglars break in and steal. Instead, store up for yourselves wealth in heaven, where neither moth nor rust destroys, and burglars do not break in or steal. For where your wealth is, there your heart will be also."*

This passage contains some of the most revolutionary teachings of our Lord – and some of the most neglected. The theme of the rest of the chapter is how to find security for the future.

In these verses, Yeshua goes against all human advice to provide for a financially secure future. When he says, *"Do not store up for yourselves wealth here on earth,"* He is indicating that there is no security in material things. Any type of material treasure on earth can be either destroyed by elements of nature or stolen by thieves. Yeshua says that the only investments not subject to loss are treasures in heaven.

This radical financial policy is based on the underlying principle that where your treasure is, there your heart is as well. If your money is in a safe-deposit box, then your heart and desire are there as well. If your treasures are in heaven, your interests will be centered there. This teaching forces us to decide whether Yeshua meant what He said or not. If He did, then we face the question, What are we going to do with our earthly treasures? If He didn't, then we face the question, What are we going to do with our Bible? Granted, we do live in a very different society and world than spoken about here in the first century. And although some saving may be necessary today, the overall principle of storing up treasures in heaven is undeniable.

Luke 6:38 says, *"Give, and you will receive gifts – the full measure, compacted, shaken together and overflowing, will be put right in your lap. For the measure with which you measure out will be used to measure back to you!"*

Love manifests itself in giving (see John 3:16; Ephesians 5:25). The believer's ministry is a ministry of expenditure. Those who give generously are rewarded generously. The picture is of a man with a large apron-like fold in the front of his garment. He uses it for carrying seed. The more widely he broadcasts the seed, the greater his harvest. He is rewarded with good measure, pressed down, shaken together, and running over. He receives it into the fold of his garment. It is a fixed principle in life that we reap according to our sowing, that our actions react upon us, and that the same measure we use on others is measured back to us. If we sow material things, we reap spiritual treasures of inestimable value. It is also true that what we keep we lose, and what we give we have.

Sometimes a person may plant a tree and never get to sit in its shade. Does the tree become a great blessing to others? Yes. Does the planter of the tree receive reward? Yes, he does. Is the reward in financial means? No; however, not only does the planter get to emulate and experience the joy in giving, but he also has for himself rewards waiting for him at the judgment seat of Messiah – a meeting that all believers will attend.

Psalm 112:5 says, *Things go well with the person who is merciful and lends, who conducts his affairs with fairness.* Things go better for the man who is generous and who doesn't refuse to lend to others who are in genuine need. This man manages his business with discretion and justice. His life is built on a stable foundation, and he will be remembered long after he is gone.

This principle of giving and generosity is unfailingly clear; we cannot out-give our gracious Creator. In fact, the only place in the Bible where God invites Israel to test Him is in Malachi 3:10, where it says, *"Bring the whole tenth into the storehouse, so that there will be food in my house, and put me to the test," says ADONAI-Tzva'ot. "See if I won't open for you the floodgates of heaven and pour out for you a blessing far beyond your needs."*

This principle of giving and generosity is unfailingly clear; we cannot out-give our gracious Creator.

God promises Israel that if they will be faithful with their tithes, He will bless them with incredible plenty, so much so that there will not be room to receive it. He will deliver them from drought, plague, enemies, and locusts, and make them a blessing in the earth. Our return may not be material blessings, but the principle of God's reward still stands.

The words of Solomon echo this in Proverbs 11:24-25, which says, *Some give freely and still get richer, while others are stingy but grow still poorer. The person who blesses others will prosper; he who satisfies others will be satisfied himself.* This is a glorious paradox. We enrich ourselves by being generous. We impoverish ourselves by laying up treasures on earth. What we have, we lose. What we give, we have.

Jim Elliot said, "He is no fool who gives what he cannot keep to gain what he cannot lose."

And Dr. Barnhouse observed that everybody tithes, either to the Lord, or to the doctor, the dentist, and the garage mechanic.

The generous person reaps dividends that the miser can never know. Whatever we do for others returns to us in blessing. When a teacher prepares diligently and then teaches the class, who do you think benefits from it most – the students or the teacher?

God loves a cheerful giver; therefore, cheerful giving should be a way of life for the believer who understands the grace of God. For God so loved the world that he gave the greatest and most priceless gift ever. If we give generously, then God will watch over us and provide for us (Isaiah 58:9; Psalm 41:1-3; Proverbs 22:9; 2 Corinthians 9:8, 11). We need to remember that it's not just our treasure that we are to cheerfully give back to God, but our talents and our time as well. Our days are numbered and recorded by the divine Architect before the historic moment of our first cry (Psalm 90:12). All gifts we have are gifts from almighty God. How dare we withhold from the greatest Gift-giver ever, the very gift He has given us.

May we use our giftedness to be a blessing, as we honor the Lord with our generosity. Our cheerful giving has a magnificent result. The giver is blessed; the recipient is blessed, and the Lord is glorified. We would do well to remember that we are saved because our God so generously gave (John 3:16). As His children, we are called to be *the light of the world* (Matthew 5:14). When we trust God and honor Him by generously giving our time, treasure, and talent, we are truly letting our light shine before men, and our goodness will reflect radiantly on our Father in heaven.

I didn't know that I was plagued with attention deficit disorder, as the term wasn't really popularized when I was a child. I struggled to comprehend what I was reading. I would read a paragraph repeatedly but could not comprehend what I read. I became frustrated and decided that I could not understand what I was reading, so I made the decision not to read. Therefore, you can imagine how I felt about reading the Bible.

However, for some unbeknownst reason to me, I just loved reading the Bible. Not only was I able to understand what I was reading as I saw the words come to life and many times I would envision what was going on, but I also loved the simplicity in the way it was written. The Bible was chock-full of contrast. Not just some contrast, but extreme contrast. For instance, you have a house built on rock or a house built on sand; you either belong to the kingdom of light or you belong to the kingdom of darkness. You either sow righteousness, or you sow unrighteousness. There is the supernatural man, and there is the natural man. There are things that God loves, and things that God hates. For a simple person like me, the Bible was so welcoming to my persona. The more I read, the more I saw that the Bible was written in black and white. There were no gray areas in the Bible. The more I read, the more I realized that there were but two paths to follow in the Bible. One path leads to everlasting life, and the other path, sadly enough, leads to everlasting perdition.

I even saw great contrast the first time I visited Israel. I noticed that there were two seas in the land – the Sea of Galilee in the northern part of the country, and the Salt Sea in the southern end of the country. Both seas are fed by the Jordan River with its headwaters coming from Mount Hermon in the far north. The Jordan feeds into the Sea of Galilee, and then water from the Sea of Galilee flows south through the country all the way to the Salt Sea as its final destination. Interestingly enough, the Sea of Galilee receives water and gives water, and it is full of life. It has an abundance of fish. The Salt Sea receives water but doesn't give out any water; it is full of death. No marine life lives in the Salt Sea, which is how it got its popular name – the Dead Sea. The paradox for me was striking. We were called to be channels of God's goodness, not terminals. We live by giving; in fact, the Bible says we were made to bring forth rivers of living waters.

If we want to love the things that God loves, not only will we love the cheerful giver, but we will also become one ourselves.

John 7:38 says, *"Whoever puts his trust in me, as the Scripture says, rivers of living water will flow from his inmost being!"*

To believe on Messiah is synonymous with coming to Messiah and drinking of Him.

All those who believe in Him will have their own needs supplied and will receive rivers of spiritual blessing to pour out to others. Throughout the Old Testament, it was taught that those who accepted the Messiah would be channels of blessing to others. Rivers of living waters flowing from us means that out of a person's inward parts would flow streams of help to others. How can anyone be indwelt with the Spirit of God and keep that Spirit to himself? If we want to love the things that God loves, not only will we love the cheerful giver, but we will also become one ourselves.

CHAPTER 17

A MAN AFTER GOD'S HEART

It is one thing for almighty God to pay attention to us, and quite another thing to be considered *a man after God's heart*. Throughout the course of our lives God is paying attention to us. In fact, most of the time we don't even realize it. I can remember watching my oldest son one day when he was about one year old. I happened to be passing by with a load of laundry in my hands, and I noticed that he was standing up and tugging on a doily that was under a rather large, wrought-iron menorah that was above him on a table, which he could not see. He tugged hard, and the large, wrought-iron menorah tipped over and was coming down on his precious little head. I immediately dropped the basket of laundry, and I reached out to grab the menorah in midair. Obviously, my reflexes were much better thirty years ago. My little child had no idea of the impending danger that was coming down on his head. He just continued on his merry, oblivious way.

Once I realized that my son was safe and out of harm's way, I was relieved. I took a breath, looked up to the heavens, and thanked God for putting me at the right place at the right time. I thought how amazing it was that I just happened to be passing by at the exact same time the menorah was about to do some serious damage to my little boy, not to mention the damage that would have ensued after his mother got home. God spoke to me in that very moment and said, "Son, do you have any idea how many things are coming down on your head in the course of the day that I reach out and grab to prevent you from being hurt?" I was blown away by this revelation from the Lord. I realized at that moment that I am like my little boy: just cruising around, blind to all the potential dangers that God saves me from. As a human being, we tend to walk by sight for the most part, rather than walking by faith.

Knowing that God is intimately involved with His children every day should be comforting and assuring for us.

Knowing that God is infinitely and intimately involved with His children all day and every day should be comforting and assuring for us. It's overwhelming to think that God is this concerned about us and that He is regarding us. That would be more than enough. But as mentioned earlier, some of us are satisfied with being in the outer courtyard, or the Holy Place, for that matter. Then there are others who want to enter into the holy of holies. They want to be in God's presence. They want to be as close to God as possible. They have a desire to be known as men after God's own heart.

Acts 13:22 says, *"God removed him and raised up David as king for them, making his approval known with these words, 'I found David Ben-Yishai to be a man after my own heart; he will do everything I want.'"*

This verse combines quotations from Psalm 89:20, *"I have found David my servant and anointed him with my holy oil,"* and 1 Samuel 13:14, *"But as it is, your kingship will not be established. ADONAI has sought for himself a man after his own heart, and ADONAI has appointed him to be prince over his people, because you did not observe what ADONAI ordered you to do."* Because of his disobedience, Saul was removed from the throne, and David was raised up to replace him. God paid high tribute to David as a man after His own heart, who would do all His will.

To understand why David was a man after God's own heart, we need to see what characteristics he had to qualify him for such a highly regarded and honored description. The answer to why David was considered a man after God's own heart is found right in the verse: *"He will do everything I want."* In other words, David did whatever God wanted him to do. An obvious question is, How could God still call David a man after His own heart when David committed such terrible sins, including adultery and murder?

If you were to be marooned on a deserted island with only one book of the Bible, which one would you choose? William MacDonald said, "Well, I hope I never have to make that choice, but if I had to, I think I would choose the Psalms. Their range of subjects is so vast, their catalogue of life's experiences so full, and their worship so exalted that I would be well supplied with the rich spiritual food and powerful fuel for praise and prayer for a long time."

Graham Scroggie said, "How full of praise to God are these Psalms! The keyboard of creation, providence and redemption are all swept by the ecstatic soul; and heaven and earth, sea and sky, things animate and things inanimate are summoned to praise the Lord."[12]

The Psalms are often called the Psalms of David, but in reality, only about half (seventy-three) are directly attributed to the sweet singer of Israel. When we think of the Psalms, however, we usually do so in connection with the life of David. And Adolf Saphir expressed this beautifully: "The harp of David still sounds in our ears, and the Holy Ghost has crystalized for us the prayers and praises of the son of Jesse. Someone said that the architecture was music frosted. The Psalms are the music of the heart, sometimes plaintive and sad, sometimes joyous and jubilant, sometimes full of darkness and anguish, sometimes tranquil and happy, the music of David's soul, preserved by the Spirit that, hearing it, we may feel encouraged to draw nigh to God."[13]

When we read the Bible, God speaks *to* us, but when we read the Psalms, they speak *for* us. They are real and raw, and we learn much about David's character in the book of Psalms as he opened up his life for all to examine. David's life was a portrait of success and failure, and the biblical record highlights the fact that David was far from perfect. But what made David a cut above the rest was that his heart was pointed toward God.

---

12 W. Graham Scroggie, *Method in Prayer: An Exposition and Exhortation* (New York: George H. Doran Company, 1916), 137.

13 Adolf Saphir, *The Hidden Life: Thoughts on Communion with God* (New York: Robert Carter and Brothers, 1877), 75.

He had a deep desire to follow God's will and do *everything* God wanted him to do. He was a man after God's own heart. Let's look at some characteristics that depict this very thing.

Part of why David is called a man after God's own heart is that he had absolute faith in God. Nowhere in Scripture is this point better illustrated than in 1 Samuel 17 where David, as a young shepherd boy, fearlessly defeated the Philistine giant Goliath. The Philistines gathered their armies for battle near the Valley of Elah, southwest of Jerusalem and not far from Gath. Saul and his army assembled nearby with the Valley of Elah between them. A champion by the name of Goliath came out of the Philistine camp daily for forty days, defying the armies of Israel to send him a worthy opponent. There were no volunteers. This giant was about nine feet nine inches tall and wore at least 175 pounds of armor. His iron spearhead alone weighed over 15 pounds. The heavy weapons were no problem for Goliath, since he must have weighed between 600 and 750 pounds (possibly more, depending on his build). This gave him many times the strength of a normal man.

Part of why David is called a man after God's own heart is that he had absolute faith in God.

On one occasion, when David was bringing supplies to his three oldest brothers at the battlefront, he heard the taunts of the giant and saw the fear on the faces of the Hebrew soldiers. He asked what would be done for the man who silenced the giant. Eliab, his oldest brother, rebuked him, probably to mask his own cowardice, but David persisted in checking into the reward that awaited the man who would kill the giant. *David said to the men standing with him, "What reward will be given* to the man who kills this P'lishti and removes this disgrace from Isra'el? Who is this uncircumcised P'lishti anyway, that he challenges the armies of the living God?" (1 Samuel 17:26).

Saul soon got word that a young man had been found to fight for Israel, and David was brought before him. When Saul saw David, he had understandable doubts about his ability. But David had known the power of God working through him when he defended his flock against the lion and the bear. He had proved God in private; now he could rely on God in public. Seeing his courage and determination, Saul gave him his own armor, but David tossed it because it was a hindrance to him. Instead, he went forth armed with five smooth stones, a sling, a staff, and the power of the living God!

Shortly before the duel, we see direct evidence of David's faith: *Then David said, "ADONAI, who rescued me from the paw of the lion and from the paw of the bear, will rescue me from the paw of this P'lishti!" Sha'ul said to David, "Go; may ADONAI be with you"* (1 Samuel 17:37).

When Goliath saw David, who was probably about twenty years old at this time, he was incensed that Israel should insult him by sending out what in his eyes was a mere child to fight him. But David had no trace of fear as he responded to the giant's curses.

> *The P'lishti, with his shield-bearer ahead of him,*
> *came nearer and nearer to David. The P'lishti*
> *looked David up and down and had nothing but*
> *scorn for what he saw – a boy with ruddy cheeks,*
> *red hair and good looks. The P'lishti said to David,*

*"Am I a dog? Is that why you're coming at me with
sticks?" – and the P'lishti cursed David by his god.
Then the P'lishti said to David, "Come here to me,
so I can give your flesh to the birds in the air and the
wild animals." David answered the P'lishti, "You're
coming at me with a sword, a spear and a javelin.
But I'm coming at you in the name of* ADONAI-
Tzva'ot, *the God of the armies of Isra'el, whom you
have challenged. Today* ADONAI *will hand you
over to me. I will attack you, lop your head off,
and give the carcasses of the army of the P'lishtim
to the birds in the air and the animals in the land.
Then all the land will know that there is a God in
Isra'el, and everyone assembled here will know that*
ADONAI *does not save by sword or spear. For this is*
ADONAI's *battle, and he will hand you over to us."*
(1 Samuel 17:41-47)

David had complete faith that the Lord would give him the
victory. How else would one walk into a dual against a 750-
pound, nine-foot-nine giant who was a renown undefeated
warrior with such confidence? David knew early in life that God
was to be trusted and obeyed. As we see in Scripture, David's
faith pleased God, and God rewards David for his faithful-
ness. He is also honored in the honor roll of the faithful in the
Old Testament as an exhortation to us to be faithful to God.
*What more should I say? There isn't time to tell about Gid'on,
Barak, Shimshon, Yiftach,* **David**, *Sh'mu'el and the prophets*
(Hebrews 11:32 emphasis added).

Another reason David was a man after God's own heart is that he absolutely loved God's law. Of the 150 psalms in the Bible, David is credited with writing about half of them. Writing at various and often troubling times in his life, David repeatedly mentioned how much he loved God's perfect Word. We find a beautiful example of this in Psalm 119:47-48: *I will delight myself in your mitzvot* [commandments], *which I have loved. I will lift my hands to your mitzvot, which I love; and I will meditate on your laws.* It is not hard to see his complete adoration for God's Word. Also notice how David *meditates* on God's statutes. David loved God's law. He found deep personal enjoyment in its pages. It was a fountain of great delight, a river of pleasure, a never-failing source of satisfaction for him.

David revered the Word of God in the sense that he stood in awe of its scope, its depths, its power, its treasures, and its infinity. He loved it for what it is and for what it has done. *I praise you seven times a day because of your righteous rulings* (Psalm 119:164). Since seven is the number of perfection or completeness, we understand the psalmist to mean that he praised the Lord continually and wholeheartedly for His righteous ordinances. And he meditated on the Word of God by day and by night.

God granted David understanding and wisdom through daily meditation. We would do well to not only read God's Word but to also think about it throughout the day, for God loves it when we think about Him. *How happy are those who observe his instruction, who seek him wholeheartedly! They do nothing wrong but live by his ways* (Psalm 119:2-3). The more we meditate on the Word of God, the more we will separate ourselves from every form of iniquity. This will help us follow the route God has mapped out for us in the Scriptures. The surest way to abstain from evil is to be occupied with doing good.

David was a man after God's own heart in that he was truly thankful. *I will wash my hands in innocence and walk around your altar, ADONAI, lifting my voice in thanks and proclaiming all your wonders* (Psalm 26:6-7). David's life was marked by seasons of great peace and prosperity as well as times of fear and despair. But through all of the seasons in his life, he never forgot to thank the Lord for everything that he had – this was one of his finest characteristics. *Enter his gates with thanksgiving, enter his courtyards with praise; give thanks to him, and bless his name* (Psalm 100:4). As followers of Messiah Yeshua, we would do well to follow David's lead of offering praise through thanksgiving to our Lord. First Thessalonians 5:18 says, *In everything give thanks, for this is what God wants from you who are united with the Messiah Yeshua.* Giving thanks to God should be the believer's native emotion. If Romans 8:28 is true – *We know that God causes everything to work together for the good of those who love God and are called in accordance with his purpose* – then we should be able to praise the Lord at all times, in all circumstances, and for everything, as long as in doing so, we do not excuse sin.

Another reason David was called a man after God's heart is that after he sinned, he was truly penitent. David's sin with Bathsheba is recorded in 2 Samuel 11:2-5:

> *The more we meditate on the Word of God, the more we will separate ourselves from every form of iniquity.*

*Once, after his afternoon nap, David got up from
his bed and went strolling on the roof of the king's
palace. From the roof he saw a woman bathing, who
was very beautiful. David made inquiries about
the woman and was told that she was Bat-Sheva
the daughter of Eli'am, the wife of Uriyah the Hitti.
David sent messengers to get her, and she came to
him, and he went to bed with her (for she had been
purified from her uncleanness). Then she returned
to her house. The woman conceived; and she sent a
message to David, "I am pregnant."*

The mighty fall hard, and David's fall included adultery, lying,
and murder. In fact, if we look at the things God hates in
Proverbs 6:16-19 – *a haughty look, a lying tongue, hands that
shed innocent blood, a heart that plots wicked schemes, feet swift
in running to do evil, a false witness who lies with every breath,
and him who sows strife among brothers* – David actually nailed
all seven of them in one fell swoop.

David had sinned against God, and he admits it in
2 Samuel 12:13. *David said to Natan, "I have sinned against
ADONAI." Natan said to David, "ADONAI also has taken away
your sin. You will not die."* We must take responsibility for our
own actions without qualification. *When I acknowledged my
sin to you, when I stopped concealing my guilt, and said, "I will
confess my offenses to ADONAI"; then you, you forgave the guilt
of my sin* (Psalm 32:5). Do you notice the word before *sin, guilt,*
and *offenses*? ***My*** *sin;* ***my*** *guilt;* ***my*** *offenses* (emphasis added). But

admitting our sin and asking for forgiveness is only half of the equation. The other half is repentance, and David did that as well.

Psalm 51 is David's prayer of repentance to God. *When Natan the prophet came to him after his affair with Bat-Sheva: God, in your grace, have mercy on me; in your great compassion, blot out my crimes. Wash me completely from my guilt, and cleanse me from my sin* (Psalm 51:1-2).

Alexander Maclaren once said, "The alchemy of divine love can extract sweet perfumes of penitence and praise out of the filth of sin."

Psalm 26:8 says, *ADONAI, I love the house where you live, the place where your glory abides.* To David, worship was not a dreary ritual to be endured stoically; he actually loved the house of the Lord where the glory cloud symbolized the glorious presence of God Himself.

Psalm 122:1 says, *I was glad when they said to me, "The house of ADONAI! Let's go!"* David caught the scent of that pure delight when the reminder was passed to him by God-fearing Jews that it was time to go to the feast in Jerusalem. He was glad. It was no burdensome duty or dreary routine. In going to the temple to worship, he found fulfillment and joy. It is crucial for those who attend worship services to *enter his gates with thanksgiving, enter his courtyards with praise; give thanks to him, and bless his name* (Psalm 100:4). This is attractive to God.

> To David, worship was not a dreary ritual to be endured stoically; he actually loved the house of the Lord.

When David wandered in exile at Engedi during the rebellion of his own son Absalom, he was estranged from the temple.

In Psalm 42:1-5, he cried out, *Just as a deer longs for running streams, God, I long for you. I am thirsty for God, for the living God! When can I come and appear before God? My tears are my food, day and night, while all day people ask me, "Where is your God?" I recall, as my feelings well up within me, how I'd go with the crowd to the house of God, with sounds of joy and praise from the throngs observing the festival.*

Who can describe the bitterness of estrangement from the Lord? It is like a continual diet of tears, a life of unalleviated misery. Then of course there is the memory of better days, the remembrance of how wonderful it was to walk in unbroken fellowship with God that makes the absence of this fellowship so intolerable. John Knox captured the mood of verse 4 when he said, "Memories come back to me yet, melting the heart: how once I would join with the throng, leading the way to God's house, amid cries of joy and thanksgiving, and all the bustle of holiday."

David was a man after God's own heart because he demonstrated his faith and was committed to following the Lord. Yes, his faith was tested on a grand scale, and he failed at times; but after his sin, he sought and received the Lord's forgiveness. In the final analysis, David loved God's law and sought to follow it exactly. The more we hate the things that God hates and the more we love the things that God loves, the more we will be like David, a man after God's heart.

CHAPTER 18

THE GOSPEL ACCORDING
TO ISAIAH

It is significant that the first chapter of the evangelical prophet, whose name means "the salvation of God," should contain the winning gospel invitation: *"Come now," says* ADONAI, *"let's talk this over together. Even if your sins are like scarlet, they will be white as snow; even if they are red as crimson, they will be like wool"* (Isaiah 1:18).

Divine reasoning, accepted by faith, teaches that there is cleansing from sin, that this cleansing is totally apart from human merit or effort, and that it is only through the redemption that the Lord Yeshua accomplished by the shedding of His blood on the cross. Who can fathom the multitudes of people who have said yes to the invitation of Isaiah 1:18? And it is still sounding out today! What a good and gracious God to extend such a glorious and merciful invitation to subjects who have shunned and even rebelled against Him. Who is this great and gracious God? He is none other than the Lord of Lords and the King of Kings, high and lifted up.

Isaiah 6:1-5, says,

> *In the year of King 'Uziyahu's death I saw Adonai*
> *sitting on a high, lofty throne! The hem of his robe*
> *filled the temple. S'rafim stood over him, each with*
> *six wings – two for covering his face, two for cover-*
> *ing his feet and two for flying. They were crying out*
> *to each other, "More holy than the holiest holiness*
> *is ADONAI-Tzva'ot! The whole earth is filled with his*
> *glory!" The doorposts shook at the sound of their*
> *shouting, and the house was filled with smoke. Then*
> *I said, "Woe to me! I [too] am doomed! – because I,*
> *a man with unclean lips, living among a people with*
> *unclean lips, have seen with my own eyes the King,*
> *ADONAI-Tzva'ot!"*

Isaiah had a vision of the King of Kings. We learn from John 12:39-41 that the King whom he saw was none other than the Lord Yeshua. *The reason they could not believe was – as Yesha'yahu [Isaiah] said elsewhere – "He has blinded their eyes and hardened their hearts, so that they do not see with their eyes, understand with their hearts, and do t'shuvah [repentance], so that I could heal them." (Yesha'yahu said these things because he saw the Sh'khinah [Glory] of Yeshua and spoke about him.)*

Isaiah sees the Lord in majestic splendor, sitting on a throne high and exalted, for His throne rules over all. Attending Him were celestial beings called seraphim with four wings for reverence and two for service. These celebrate the holiness of God and require that God's servants be cleansed before serving Him. The vision produced deep conviction of sin in the prophet and brought him to the place of confession. The first step in a relationship with God is acknowledging our lawlessness. We have to come to grips with who we are and who we're not, in order to comprehend the Lord's glory and goodness.

We have to come to grips with who we are and who we're not, in order to comprehend the Lord's glory and goodness.

Isaiah 59:1-8 says,

> ADONAI's arm is not too short to save, nor is his ear too dull to hear. Rather, it is your own crimes that separate you from your God; your sins have hidden his face from you, so that he doesn't hear. For your hands are stained with blood and your fingers with crime; your lips speak lies, your tongues utter wicked things. No one sues with just cause, no one pleads honestly in court, they trust in empty words and say worthless things; they conceive trouble and give birth to evil. They hatch viper eggs and spin spiderwebs; whoever eats their eggs dies, and the crushed egg hatches a snake. Their webs are useless as clothing, their deeds are useless for wearing; their deeds are deeds of wickedness, their hands produce violence. Their feet run to evil, they rush to shed

innocent blood, their thoughts are thoughts of wickedness, their paths lead to havoc and ruin. The way of shalom they do not know, their goings-about obey no law, they make devious paths for themselves; no one treading them will ever know shalom.

Israel's sin holds God back from delivering them; the fault cannot be laid at God's door. Their hands, fingers, lips, and tongue are all active in murder and lying. There is widespread perversion of justice and dishonesty. People conceive evil and bring forth crime. Their activities are as dangerous as vipers' eggs and as useless as a spider's web. Sin controls every area of their lives – what they do, where they go, what they think. They care nothing for peace and justice, preferring what is crooked. What was true of Israel is also true of the entire human race: *"Their feet rush to shed blood, in their ways are ruin and misery, and the way of shalom they do not know"* (Romans 3:15-17).

Chapter 3 in the book of Romans discusses the universal need for the gospel, for all people are under the power of sin. Romans 3:10-11 says, *As the Tanakh puts it, "There is no one righteous, not even one! No one understands, no one seeks God."* These verses are from Psalm 14:1-2 and clearly declare that if left to his own devices, fallen man would never seek God. It is only by God's grace, through the power of the Holy Spirit, that anyone ever does. Some will say, "I've found the Lord." As well intentioned as that statement may be, the fact remains that *they* were lost, not God.

Romans 3:11 and Psalm 14:2 say that all men have gone astray from God. All mankind has become corrupt. There is not one who lives a good life, no, not one. Some think they are good, but it can't be so. The problem is that most people compare themselves to Jack the Ripper, as opposed to Yeshua the Messiah. Being good means not being bad, and there is only One who can ever state that claim.

> *Therefore, since we have a great cohen gadol* [high priest] *who has passed through to the highest heaven, Yeshua, the Son of God, let us hold firmly to what we acknowledge as true. For we do not have a cohen gadol unable to empathize with our weaknesses; since in every respect he was tempted just as we are, the only difference being that he did not sin* (Hebrews 4:14-15).

Then in Romans 3:13-14, Paul uses the *Tanakh* (Old Testament) once again when he says, *"Their throats are open graves, they use their tongues to deceive. Vipers' venom is under their lips. Their mouths are full of curses and bitterness."* Men's throats are like an open tomb. Their speech has been consistently and deceitfully used to devour their victims. They are habitual and insincere flatterers. *For in their mouths there is nothing sincere, within them are calamities, their throats are open tombs, they flatter with their tongues* (Psalm 5:9). Their conversations flow from poisonous lips. Their words spew deadly poison. *They have made their tongues as sharp as a snake's; viper's venom is under their lips* (Psalm 140:3).

Then Paul uses the *Tanakh* even further to drive the point home, as he quotes from Isaiah 59:7-8 in Romans 3:15-17.

"*Their feet rush to shed blood, in their ways are ruin and misery, and the way of shalom they do not know.*" And he ends with Romans 3:18, which is a direct quote from Psalm 36:1. "*There is no fear of God before their eyes.*" The bottom line is that men have no respect for God. The sinner abandons any fear of God.

Some men think maybe we can begin to offset or even abrogate our sin with works of righteousness. They think, if our good works outweigh our bad works, then not only will we neutralize our bad works, but we will also have a credit balance in our spiritual life account. We will come up good before God, and therefore He will have to save us. Although this seems to be a logical approach, it is not the way. I once asked a rabbi the following question: "How does one get to heaven?"

His answer was, "We just have to make sure our good works outweigh our bad ones."

I then asked, "How do we know if our good works outweigh our bad ones?" I talked to him about sins of commission, sins of omission, premediated sins, unintentional sins, secret sins, and sins we don't know are sins. I then tried to use the *Tanakh*, focusing on the book of Isaiah. I used Isaiah 59:2, Isaiah 64:6, and Isaiah 53, of course. However, like so many others don't realize that they are sinners in need of a Savior, he simply didn't see it.

Isaiah 64:6 says, *All of us are like someone unclean, all our righteous deeds like menstrual rags; we wither, all of us, like leaves; and our misdeeds blow us away like the wind.* Here the people confess their personal uncleanness and admit that their best deeds (acts of righteousness) are like filthy rags, in particular, menstrual rags. No wonder they are fading leaves, driven away by the wind of their iniquities. Isaiah tells the people that there is spiritual deadness in Israel. Intercessors are nowhere to be found, because God has abandoned them to the consequences of their sins. Oh, dear God, we desperately need a Savior. We need someone or something that can bridge the gap that has been created between sinful man on earth, and a holy God in heaven.

Therefore Adonai himself will give you people a sign: the young woman will become pregnant, bear a son and name him 'Immanu El [God is with us] (Isaiah 7:14). This verse points irresistibly to Messiah Yeshua, the Son of the Virgin whose name indicates that He is Immanuel, (God with us). The choice of the Hebrew word *almah* for *young woman* is significant, as it is distinct from the Hebrew word *bethulah* (a maiden living with her parents and whose marriage was not impending).

> *We need someone that can bridge the gap that has been created between sinful man and a holy God.*

Almah denotes one who is mature, a virgin, and ready for marriage. Isaiah is pointing us to none other than the God-man, prophesied over three hundred times in the Old Testament, who will bridge the gap between sinful men on earth and a holy God in heaven. But who is this savior of men?

> *For a child is born to us, a son is given to us; dominion will rest on his shoulders, and he will be given the name Pele-Yo'etz El Gibbor Avi-'Ad Sar-Shalom [Wonder of a Counselor, Mighty God, Father of Eternity, Prince of Peace], in order to extend the dominion and perpetuate the peace of the throne and kingdom of David, to secure it and sustain*

*it through justice and righteousness henceforth
and forever. The zeal of ADONAI-Tzva'ot [Lord of
Heaven's armies] will accomplish this.* (Isaiah 9:6-7)

The first advent is described in verse 6: *For a child is born to
us, a son is given to us.* The first clause speaks of His humanity, the second of His deity. The next part of the verse points
forward to the second advent: He will reign as King of Kings
and Lord of Lords. His name is a noun, not an adjective, and
speaks of His person and His work. His wisdom is infinitely
great in government. He is the omnipotent Supreme Ruler, and
the Father or source of all eternity. Eternal Himself, He bestows
eternal life as a gift on those who believe in Him. He not only
inhabits and possesses eternity, but He is also loving, tender,
compassionate, all-wise Instructor, Trainer, and Provider. His
is the Prince of Peace, the One who will at last bring peace to
this troubled, twisted world. His government will be extensive,
peaceful, and endless. Sitting upon the throne of David, He will
rule with judgment and justice. How will all this be brought
about? The Lord's jealous care for His people will do it.

> *"See how my servant will succeed! He will be
> raised up, exalted, highly honored! Just as many
> were appalled at him, because he was so disfig-
> ured that he didn't even seem human and simply
> no longer looked like a man, so now he will startle
> many nations; because of him, kings will be speech-
> less. For they will see what they had not been told,*

they will ponder things they had never heard."
(Isaiah 52:13-15)

God's servant dealt wisely throughout His earthly ministry. He was exalted in resurrection, lifted up in ascension, and made high in glory at God's right hand. At His first coming, many were shocked at the depths of His suffering. His face and His body were marred beyond recognition as a man. But when He comes a second time, men will be shocked once again, but this time it will be in regards to the magnificence of His glory. Gentile kings will be speechless when they see His unheard-of and incomparable splendor. They will understand then that the humble Man of Golgotha is none other than the King of Kings and Lord of Lords. But first He had to go to the cross:

For before him he grew up like a young plant, like a root out of dry ground. He was not well-formed or especially handsome; we saw him, but his appearance did not attract us. People despised and avoided him, a man of pains, well acquainted with illness. Like someone from whom people turn their faces, he was despised; we did not value him. In fact, it was our diseases he bore, our pains from which he suffered; yet we regarded him as punished, stricken and afflicted by God. But he was wounded because of our crimes, crushed because of our sins; the disciplining that makes us whole fell on him, and by his bruises we are healed. We all, like sheep, went astray; we turned, each one, to his own way; yet

ADONAI laid on him the guilt of all of us. Though mistreated, he was submissive – he did not open his mouth. Like a lamb led to be slaughtered, like a sheep silent before its shearers, he did not open his mouth. After forcible arrest and sentencing, he was taken away; and none of his generation protested his being cut off from the land of the living for the crimes of my people, who deserved the punishment themselves. He was given a grave among the wicked; in his death he was with a rich man. Although he had done no violence and had said nothing deceptive, yet it pleased ADONAI to crush him with illness, to see if he would present himself as a guilt offering. If he does, he will see his offspring; and he will prolong his days; and at his hand ADONAI's desire will be accomplished. After this ordeal, he will see satisfaction. "By his knowing [pain and sacrifice], my righteous servant makes many righteous; it is for their sins that he suffers." (Isaiah 53:2-11)

Hallelujah!

For those of us who choose to accept this truth and say yes to this glorious invitation for salvation, we can make Isaiah 61:10 our own: *I am so joyful in ADONAI! My soul rejoices in my God, for he has clothed me in salvation, dressed me with a robe of triumph, like a bridegroom wearing a festive turban, like a bride adorned with her jewels.*

The Messiah leads the praises of His redeemed remnant. He celebrates the glorious garments of salvation and righteousness with which God has decked them, and the beauty and sanctity of practical righteousness. Now we come back to where this all began:

> "Heaven is my throne," says ADONAI, "and the earth is my footstool. What kind of house could you build for me? What sort of place could you devise for my rest? Didn't I myself make all these things? This is how they all came to be," says ADONAI. "The kind of person on whom I look with favor is one with a poor and humble spirit, who trembles at my word." (Isaiah 66:1-2)

Because of all the grace and mercy that the Lord bestowed upon us, we want to be as near to this great God and Savior as possible. So here in Isaiah 66:1-2, the prophet tells us how: namely, to depend on Him, to trust Him, to not be full of ourselves, but to be full of our need for Him, to not think less of ourselves, but to think less about ourselves. And this is all accomplished by hating what He hates, and loving what He loves.

Because of all the grace that the Lord bestowed upon us, we want to be as near to this great God as possible.

THE CONCLUSION

Isaiah 59:2 says, *It is your own crimes that separate you from your God; your sins have hidden his face from you, so that he doesn't hear.* This is what the prophet Isaiah spoke to Israel regarding her iniquities. And it is true for us as well. Sin is any thought, word, or deed that falls short of God's standard of holiness and perfection. An Indian whose arrow fell short of its target was heard to say, "Oh, I sinned." In his language, the same word was used to express sinning and falling short of the target.

Sin is lawlessness (1 John 3:4), the rebellion of the creature's will against the will of God. Sin is not only doing what is wrong, but it is also the failure to do what one knows to be right (James 4:17). Whatever is not of faith is sin (Romans 14:23). This means that it is wrong for a man to do anything about which he has a reasonable doubt. If he does not have a clear conscience about it and yet goes ahead and does it, he is sinning.

A very simple way to define sin is that when we sin, we are *going against the ways of God*. When you and I go against something, we are in essence separating ourselves from it. Therefore, by definition, when we sin, we go against God and disconnect ourselves from Him.

Sadly enough, even as believers, we still sin at times and find ourselves estranged from God. Sin is like a dark curtain pulled over a sunny window. The sun is still there, but the curtain creates a separation from its beauty, warmth, and light. There are basically two kinds of sins: sins of commission and sins of omission. A sin of commission is a sin we take action to commit, whether in thought, word, or deed. Sins of omission are those in which we knew we should have done something good, but refused. When we do the things that God hates, we are committing sins of commission, and when we don't do the things that God loves, we are committing sins of omission.

> *Sin is like a curtain pulled over a sunny window. The sun is still there, but the curtain creates a separation from its light.*

Proverbs 6:16-19 (NLT) says, *There are six things the Lord hates—no, seven things he detests: haughty eyes, a lying tongue, hands that kill the innocent, a heart that plots evil, feet that race to do wrong, a false witness who pours out lies, a person who sows discord in a family.*

To be perfectly frank, when I first read this list, I was quite familiar with it. In fact, for the most part, these were the things I used to do. Thank God for His tender loving mercy and His amazing grace, whereby He saved a wretch like me. He changed my heart, filled me with His Spirit, and created in me a real desire not to do the things He hates any longer. Things that I used to do, I stopped doing, and things that I never thought I would be doing, I am in fact doing. I was born again! I had a new heart with a new spirit, and thus I became a new man. This new man started to live a life doing things that pleased the Lord. Truth be told, for the first time in my life, I was truly happy, and for the first time in my life, I knew peace. To God be the glory, the honor, and the power, forever and ever.

Then I discovered the things that God loves: namely, God loves people; He loves sinners, and He loves all believers. He loves those who do right; He loves those who treat others fairly; He loves those who obey His Word; and He loves a cheerful giver. When we don't do these things, we are committing sins of omission. Sins of omission tend to go a bit under the radar, since they are more stealthlike. I believe it is easier to see when a person is doing the things that God hates than to see when a person is not doing the things that God loves. A person can be conscientious about not doing the things that God hates, but at the same time, he may be indifferent about doing the things that God loves.

We must remember that we were all once enemies of God, but in God's infinite love, wisdom, grace, and mercy, He drew near to us. Thankfully, He didn't stand at a distance, but He came from heaven to earth and paid the ultimate price to a world that not only shunned Him but cursed Him as well. He was heaven's best for earth's worst, and in spite of it all, Yeshua cried out, *"Father, forgive them"* (Luke 23:34).

When all the theology is said and done, if we call ourselves believers, and we claim the forgiveness of our sins through the shed blood of Yeshua, then our one and only goal is to become as much like Yeshua as possible. This fact crosses all ethnic, cultural, and denominational lines. Yeshua not only hated what God hated and loved what God loved, but He also embodies it.

Yeshua is the antithesis of the things that God hates. For instance, He was the essence of humility. He never lied, and the only thing He murdered was our sins. His heart plotted good always, and His feet raced to do righteousness. He was the faithful witness who poured out truth and sowed harmony not only in natural families but in God's family as well.

If we look at the list of the things that God loves, it describes Yeshua to a tee. For instance, He loves people; He loves sinners; and He loves believers. He loves those who do right; He loves those who treat others fairly; and He loves those that obey His Word. He not only loves a cheerful giver, but He shall also go down in history as the most cheerful giver of all time, because He gave Himself to an undeserving world. May we never forget that we did all the sinning, and He did all the saving!

As a parent, one can only imagine what it would feel like if one of our children were to say to us, "Dad/Mom, I love you so much, and I will do my very best to do the things you love and not do the things you hate." This would be music to the ears of any parent. Well then, why wouldn't our heavenly Father feel the same way if we were to say to Him, "Father, I love you so much, and I will do my very best to do the things you love and not do the things you hate."

I remember being totally overwhelmed on the Transfiguration Mount when I received the revelation of what God had done for me through the crucifixion of His one and only Son Yeshua.

I really couldn't handle the reality of it all. I felt so loved, and yet at the same time, so undeserving.

Soon thereafter, I remember meeting a former Catholic priest, who became an Episcopalian minister. Through my tears I told him that I had a burning desire to pay some kind of penance to God as a way of paying Him back for what He had done for me. He smiled and said, "Greg, there will be many times in your life when you will experience pain and sorrow; just enjoy the Lord."

Well, that was over thirty years ago, and you know what? He was right. I didn't get the message at the time, so I spent years and years trying to pay God back. I now realize that not only is it impossible to pay God back, but He also never asked us to. What he has asked of us is to love Him with our whole heart and to pay Him forward. I absolutely believe one of the best ways to love God with all our heart and to pay Him forward is to simply love what He loves and hate what He hates. Not only will this please the Lord, but it will get His attention as well, and He will look upon us with favor.

I believe one of the best ways to love God with all our heart is to simply love what He loves and hate what He hates.

After I met the Lord in 1989, all I wanted to do was to tell everyone and anyone about Him. I had times of joy and happiness with friends and family, but I found my highest joy was in sharing with others the goodness and greatness of our Lord. All I wanted to do was to work for Him. So I went on a quest to become a man of the cloth. I was able to meet with a bishop of an entire diocese in the state of Florida in order to enter into seminary. After the meeting, his thoughts were that I was very in love with God and very zealous about the things of God, but I was not priestly material. I was disappointed; however, I realized this was a seasoned man of God, who knew how to discern these things, so I received it and continued to work for the Lord as a lay leader in evangelism, Bible study, and youth and prison ministry.

In 1993 I stumbled on Messianic Judaism, where Jews and Gentiles worship the God of Abraham, Isaac, and Jacob through the prophesied Messiah, the Lord Yeshua, in more of a first-century Hebraic flavor. Little did I know it would be my calling for the rest of my days – to help bridge the gap between traditional Judaism and traditional Christianity.

Sadly enough, a few years later, our beloved leader at our synagogue in Florida fell from grace, and the synagogue suffered a great loss. He has since been restored, for God is good! At the time though, no one was available to take over, and things were looking pretty dismal and dark. The elders came to me and asked if I would step in for the time being. I asked them if I could have some time to pray and ask the Lord if this was His will.

In the midst of seeking God, He told me that He had actually ordained this position for me. I asked Him, if He did, then why was I told that I wasn't priestly material? God said that He had blocked my way from going into seminary. I was confused and thought to myself, Why would you do that, Lord? God answered that He wanted a man after His own heart. He wanted someone who would just trust and obey Him. He wanted a man that was raw that He could lead. Now I am not intimating that going to seminary is a bad thing. I have friends that are seminarians, and they are wonderful servants of the Lord. The point is that God is looking for men and woman who will just play follow-the-leader.

One of the best ways to be a man after God's heart without exceptions is to love what He loves and to hate what He hates. The more we do this, the more pleasing we will be to God and the more He will look upon us with favor. Hopefully one day I will arrive. I hope and pray we all will. Until that day, 'Y'varekh'kha ADONAI v'yishmerekha (May ADONAI bless you and keep you). Ya'er ADONAI panav eleikha vichunekka (ADONAI make his face shine on you and show you his favor).

Yissa ADONAI panav eleikha v'yasem l'kha shalom (May ADONAI lift up his face toward you and give you peace).

ABOUT THE AUTHOR

Rabbi Greg Hershberg was born in New York City and raised in Orthodox Judaism. He graduated Pace University, Magna Cum Laude and later owned and operated an executive search firm in New York City, specializing in banking and finance. In 1989, he married Bernadette and while on his honeymoon in Israel had a visitation from the Lord that turned his heart to serving God.

In 1992, Rabbi Greg became involved in the Messianic Jewish Movement and was ordained through the International Association of Messianic Congregations and Synagogues (IAMCS). He became the leader of Beth Judah Messianic

Congregation. In 2002, the Lord moved Rabbi Greg and his family to Macon, Georgia, to lead Congregation Beth Yeshua.

The ministry went global in 2010 and Congregation Beth Yeshua became Beth Yeshua International (BYI). What was a local storefront congregation became an international ministry/training center in Macon, Georgia, with congregations and schools in India, Kenya, Ethiopia, Australia, Germany, Israel, and across America. In addition, Rabbi Greg's messages are live-streamed throughout the world.

Rabbi Greg currently resides in Macon, Georgia, with his wife, Bernadette, and their four children. More about Rabbi Greg can be found in his autobiography, *From The Projects To The Palace*.

www.bethyeshuainternational.com